A Touchstone Book

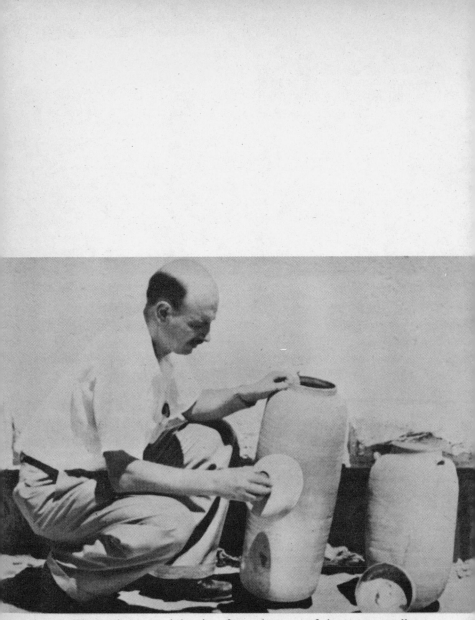

The author examining jars from the cave of the seven scrolls

THE MESSAGE
OF
THE SCROLLS

BY YIGAEL YADIN

*Lecturer in Archaeology at the
Hebrew University, Jerusalem*

A Touchstone Book
Published by
SIMON AND SCHUSTER

TO CARMELLA

Without whose insistence and assistance
this book would never have been written

Acknowledgements

I record my thanks to the following for permission to quote extracts from their publications: The American Schools of Oriental Research, Yale, *The Dead Sea Scrolls of St Mark's Monastery* by Millar Burrows, and an article in *The Biblical Archaeologist* by John C. Trever; *The New Yorker*, an article 'The Scrolls from the Dead Sea' by Edmund Wilson; the Friends of Dr William's Library, *The Hebrew Scrolls* by G. R. Driver; the Clarendon Press, *Books and Readers in Ancient Greece and Rome* by Frederick Kenyon; the British Academy, *The Cairo Geniza* by Paul E. Kahle; the Union of American Hebrew Congregations, *The Septuagint, the Oldest Translation of the Bible* by Professor Harry M. Orlinsky; and the publishers of the *Journal of Biblical Literature*, an article by John Allegro.

Y.Y.

Contents

List of Illustrations

Preface

THIS year marks the tenth anniversary of the discovery of the Dead Sea Scrolls. Several books have already been written on the subject and numerous scientific papers have seen the light in learned journals. All offer evidence of the intense interest which the discoveries have aroused both among Biblical scholars, historians and theologians throughout the world and in the general public in many countries.

This book is not intended primarily for the specialist scholar, but for the reader with an interest in the Bible and in the history of the Jewish people and of Christianity. It seeks to answer many of the questions which I have often been asked in my lectures—questions on the discovery of the scrolls, their contents, and their religious, social, and historical significance.

The general reader is somewhat baffled at the moment by conflicting theories about the origin, interpretation and meaning of these ancient manuscripts. At the present stage of research, few scholars agree on the scientific conclusions to be drawn from the writings. To present a woven fabric of fact, hypothesis and theory can only confuse the lay reader who should be permitted to distinguish between all three. The presentation of theory as fact, on such delicate or sacred matters, may be disturbing to many.

The first purpose of this book is to present all the relevant facts relating to the Dead Sea Scrolls in a straightforward manner so that the reader can draw his own conclusions. Take, as an example, the problem of the identity of the Dead Sea sect. There is evidence suggesting its identification with the sect of the Essenes, but decisive proof is lacking. If, therefore, the sect is referred to in some publications as the Essenes, the reader may be misled. It has seemed to me more appro-

11

priate to mention the facts which suggest a connexion between the two and their possible identity. I have accordingly described the principles of the organization of the Dead Sea sect as they can be inferred from their writings, and I have added the principles of the organization of the Essenes as they are known to us from historical sources. But I leave it to the reader to judge for himself as to whether they are identical.

There is a similar danger of misguiding the lay reader if one seeks at this stage to reach dogmatic conclusions on the exact influence on Christianity exercised by the teachings of the Dead Sea sect. There is no doubt of course that this sect was a completely Jewish sect—although it differed somewhat from the prevailing Judaism of Jerusalem. It is also clear that a direct or indirect affinity may be detected between some of its creeds, customs and beliefs and those which were absorbed by Christianity in its early period. But it seems to me proper to present the facts and permit the reader to reach his own conclusions. It is thus the purpose of this book to offer the reader possession of the most important facts concerning the Dead Sea Scrolls. Thus equipped, he can make up his own mind and take a critical stand on the scholars' numerous conflicting theories.

The second object of this book is to provide the reader with a full and detailed account of the discovery of the seven complete Dead Sea Scrolls and their acquisition. For reasons which will be found in the first part of the book many details of that story remained secret. This has led some scholars to doubt the antiquity of the scrolls. The literature so far published describes the story only in part. It was my father, the late Professor E. L. Sukenik, who first recognized the antiquity and the significance of the scrolls. It was he who bought the first three complete manuscripts for the Hebrew University. From his diary I have drawn the details, some of which are now published for the first time, of how he was given a clue to the existence of the scrolls and what preceded their purchase. I was lucky enough to have some share in the acquisition of the

12

remaining four complete scrolls by a fortuitous visit to the United States when they were made available for sale. These two descriptions complement, I believe, the accounts now known in both the scholarly and the lay world.

The third and possibly the most important purpose of this book is to provide a description of each separate scroll and its contents. In this way the reader with a specific interest in any one scroll will find all the details of that scroll concentrated in a single chapter.

My task has been simplified since I happen to have been the first to engage in research and deciphering of two of the seven scrolls—the War of the Sons of Light against the Sons of Darkness, and the Apocryphal Genesis. A summary of both studies is here published in English for the first time. The War manuscript is to my mind so important to the understanding of the Dead Sea sect and their way of life that it is impossible to reach any definite conclusions about the sect without a thorough study of this scroll. This is also true to some extent of the Apocryphal Genesis which sheds important light on Apocryphal literature and the Aramaic language on the eve of the birth of Christianity.

Since I have written this book with the general reader in mind I have permitted myself several observations on Biblical manuscripts in general which may be unknown to those who are not Biblical scholars. I have however limited myself only to those references without which it is difficult to grasp the significance of certain aspects of the scrolls.

One chapter in the book is devoted to a description of the excavations which uncovered not only the caves in which the scrolls were kept but also public buildings of the Dead Sea sect. I hope this will enable the reader to visualize more easily the way of life of this fascinating group of people who lived in the harsh wilderness bordering the shores of the Dead Sea.

Some of the illustrations in this book are new and are published here for the first time.

I cannot avoid the feeling that there is something symbolic in the discovery of the scrolls and their acquisition at the moment of the creation of the State of Israel. It is as if these manuscripts had been waiting in caves for two thousand years, ever since the destruction of Israel's independence, until the people of Israel had returned to their home and regained their freedom. This symbolism is heightened by the fact that the first three scrolls were bought by my father for Israel on 29th November, 1947, the very day on which the United Nations voted for the re-creation of the Jewish state in Israel after two thousand years. These facts may have influenced my approach to the scrolls. It was a tremendously exciting experience, difficult to convey in words, to see the original scrolls and to study them, knowing that some of the Biblical manuscripts were copied only a few hundred years after their composition, and that these very scrolls were read and studied by our forefathers in the period of the Second Temple. They constitute a vital link—long lost and now regained—between those ancient times, so rich in civilized thought, and the present day. And just as a Christian reader must be moved by the knowledge that here he has a manuscript of a sect whom the early Christians may have known and by whom they may have been influenced, so an Israeli and a Jew can find nothing more deeply moving than the study of manuscripts written by the People of the Book in the Land of the Book more than two thousand years ago.

PART I

CHAPTER 1

Discovery:
The Hebrew University

IN LATE November 1947, in what had once been a quiet suburb of Jerusalem, I first heard of the Dead Sea Scrolls. I was at the time Chief of Operations of Haganah, the Jewish underground self-defence movement in Palestine. My headquarters were near Tel-Aviv. On the 28th of November I went to Jerusalem to check on the preparedness of the Jewish population against possible Arab attack.

Six thousand miles away, at Lake Success, United Nations deliberations were leading up to a resolution ending the British Mandate and recommending the establishment of a Jewish State. The Resolution was to be voted on any day. Our underground intelligence reported that Arab attacks on Jewish cities and settlements throughout the country were almost certain to follow. The defence problem in Jerusalem was not easy, for there was a highly mixed Arab and Jewish population. I had come to the city for a first-hand inspection of the situation.

I spent several hours at the underground Jerusalem Haganah Headquarters, toured the city with the Haganah commander, and just before returning to Tel-Aviv I went to visit my parents. My father, Elazar L. Sukenik, was the Professor of Archaeology at the Hebrew University. I found him in a state of high exhilaration, eyes glowing with excitement. 'What shall I do?' he asked me after our exchange of *shaloms*. 'Shall I go to Bethlehem? I must. First thing in the morning. What do you say?'

I gathered that he had made an exciting archaeological

15

discovery but I could not guess what it was. He had returned only a few months earlier from a lecture tour in the United States and had not yet resumed digging. I hadn't the time to unravel the mystery on my own; I was due back at head-quarters. I bade my father sit down quietly and begin at the beginning. I confess that by the time he was half way through his story, problems of defence had receded from my mind and I was transported in time and place from Jerusalem, 1947, to the Dead Sea of two thousand years ago. For what had excited my father was a glimpse of the parchments which have now become famous as the Dead Sea Scrolls. He was the first scholar to recognize these parchments for what they were, the first to detect the first scroll as the most ancient surviving manuscript of the prophet Isaiah, the first to record the opinion, later confirmed by the Carbon 14 test, that it was at least a thousand years older than the earliest previously known copy and the first to acquire three of the scrolls for the Hebrew University.

What had happened came out with a rush as my father began talking, words tumbling over each other as he told this tremendous tale of what he was convinced were the most ancient Hebrew documents in the world, and which he felt were almost within his grasp. He was certain that he would succeed in acquiring them as a perpetual Jewish heritage, for he found something symbolic in the thought that this was happening at the very moment when Jewish sovereignty in Palestine was about to be restored after almost two thousand years—the very age of the parchments he had seen.

'It all started on Sunday,' he began. Sunday was the 23rd of November, five days earlier; it was now Friday. 'When I got to my office at the Hebrew University on Mount Scopus, I found a message from a friend, an Armenian dealer in antiquities, asking me to get in touch with him imme-diately. He is a most trustworthy person, and I knew that the matter must be urgent and important for him to telephone me on his day of rest. But I had lectures all the morning and my students were waiting. It was not until the afternoon that I was able to speak to him. He told me that he was most anxious to show me some items of interest. I asked him what they were, but he said he could not tell me on the telephone. He urged an early meeting. We fixed it for the next morning. The place we chose was the gateway to Military Zone B.'

The British security forces had recently divided the city into military zones, each marked off with barbed wire barriers and guarded by sentries; movement from one zone to another was possible only with an official pass, and neither my father nor his Armenian friend had one. So they had arranged to meet at the barrier dividing their two zones, and the whole momentous conversation was carried on across a barbed wire fence.

My father went on: 'When we met, my friend pulled from his briefcase a scrap of leather. He held it up for me to see. On it I noticed Hebrew script, but I could not make out the words. I asked him what it was and his story was so fascinating that I almost forgot the sickening presence of the barbed wire between us. He said that one of our mutual friends, an old Arab antiquities dealer in Bethlehem, had come to him the previous day with a tale of some Bedouin who had called on him bringing several parchment scrolls which they claimed to have found in a cave near the shores of the Dead Sea, not far from Jericho. They had offered to sell him the scrolls, but he, the Arab dealer, did not know whether they were genuine. He had therefore brought them to my Armenian friend. He, too, had no knowledge of whether they were really ancient manuscripts or a fairly recent product. He wanted to know from me whether I considered them genuine and if so whether I would be prepared to buy them for the Museum of Jewish Antiquities of the Hebrew University.

'I was in a difficult situation. If I gave him an immediate affirmative answer, I would be automatically committed to their purchase, since we had known each other long enough for each to trust the word of the other. I hesitated a few minutes, straining my eyes to peer through the loops of barbed wire in an effort to make out the letters on the scrap of leather. Strangely enough, as I gazed at the parchment, the letters began to become familiar, though I could make no immediate sense of the writing. They resembled letters which I had found on several occasions on small coffins and on ossuaries which I had discovered in and around Jerusalem, in some ancient tombs dating back to the period before the Roman destruction of the city. I had seen such letters scratched, carved and, in a few cases, painted on stone. But not until this week had I seen this particular kind of Hebrew lettering written with a pen on leather.

'My first thought was that this was possibly the work of some forger, who had conceived the idea of imitating the script on leather. But this thought stayed with me for barely a moment. As I continued to peer, my hunch became stronger and stronger that this was no forgery but the real thing. I decided to risk buying the scrolls, of which this was a fragment, for the University. I asked my Armenian friend to proceed at once to Bethlehem and bring back some more samples. I asked him to telephone me when he got back and in the meantime I would try and get a military pass so that I could visit him at his store and examine the parchments more closely.

'He telephoned me yesterday [Thursday, 27 November] to say that he had some additional fragments. I raced over to see him, entering Zone B with my newly acquired pass. I sat in his shop and tried to decipher the writing. It was written in a very good, clear hand, and resembled, even more closely than the first sample, the alphabet on the stone ossuaries. I was now more convinced than ever that these were fragments of genuine ancient scrolls. We resolved to go together to Bethlehem and start negotiations with the Arab dealer for their purchase. We arranged to go today, but I'm afraid I have been very foolish. I was so excited when I got home yesterday that your mother asked me what it was all about. I told her, and I was silly enough to add that I was going to Bethlehem today to see the Arab dealer. You should have heard her reaction. She said I was crazy even to think of making such a dangerous journey entirely through Arab territory at a moment of high tension, likely to explode at any minute with the passage of the UN resolution. And so I had to put him off for the moment, but I cannot, I cannot sit here doing nothing. What shall I do? Shall I go to Bethlehem?'

I was silent for a few minutes while my father mused aloud, his mind swinging from anxiety over Palestine and what would happen at Lake Success to anxiety over this new discovery. For years his mind had free-wheeled round the possibility of ancient Hebrew scrolls being turned up by the archaeologist's spade. He had often been asked: 'Is there any chance that excavations in Palestine, cradle of the Bible, will bring forth ancient Hebrew books which may shed further light on the Bible?' My father's answer had usually been that the humid climate of Palestine was unsuitable for the preservation of organic matter, which includes manuscripts of papyrus; leather or parchment. This opinion had been shared by every archaeologist who had ever worked in the country. My father was therefore weighing in his mind all the pros and cons as to the genuineness of the scrolls. His worries were aggravated by the responsibility he was assuming in buying them for the Hebrew University, perhaps spending public funds on a forgery.

What was I to tell him? As a student of archaeology myself, I felt that an opportunity of acquiring such priceless documents could not be missed. On the other hand, as Chief of Operations of Haganah, I knew perfectly well the dangers my father would be risking in travelling to Arab Bethlehem. And as a son I was torn between both feelings. I tried to hedge, but, before leaving, son and soldier won and I told him not to go. I bade him and my mother *shalom* and left for Tel-Aviv. Fortunately, my father disregarded my advice and next morning left for Bethlehem. But I did not discover this until later.

As I drove back to headquarters that late afternoon, I found myself infected by my father's excitement. My thoughts were a montage of a UN Assembly meeting, with a forest of hands rising in favour of the establishment of a Jewish state, a picture of Jerusalem under Arab attack, and a peaceful scene of scribes seated near caves on the shore of the Dead Sea, inscribing words of immortality on leather scrolls to be found, two thousand years later, by Bedouin chasing a stray goat. And always, as I drove, I kept coming back to my father's symbolic thought that these relics of the period just before the destruction of Jewish independence were almost within our grasp, at the very moment when our independence was about to be restored. I reached Haganah headquarters in Tel-Aviv. Within minutes I was grappling with the immediate problems of defence, poring with my colleagues over intelligence reports from all over the country, sitting with my operations staff making plans to defend isolated Jewish settlements and the populations of the cities, worrying about how to dispose our comparatively meagre forces and limited firepower to maximum advantage.

Next day was the 29th of November. On this day the United Nations passed the 'Jewish State' resolution with the necessary two-thirds majority. Everywhere there was jubilation. In New York and London, in Paris and in Johannesburg, there was dancing in the streets. In Palestine there was a song in every Jewish heart. And this joy, strong and powerful and all-absorbing, was in no way weakened by the realistic recognition that the morrow would probably bring a widespread attack.

It did. And with each day the attacks mounted, growing in scale, scope and intensity through December and the first five months of 1948. In May the Palestine Jewish leaders proclaimed the rebirth of the State of Israel. A few hours later Egyptian planes bombed Tel-Aviv, and next day came the declaration of war on Israel by seven neighbouring Arab States. This war they lost, and with Israel's victory it became known as Israel's War of Independence.

There was little opportunity during the early battles for talks with my father on his discoveries. It was more than a month after our first talk that I had the chance of seeing him. (I was visiting Jerusalem because a group of our co-operative settlements were under heavy attack by the Arab Legion.) It was only then that I found out that the day after I had left him, and on the very day that the United Nations Resolution was carried, he had, this time without telling my mother or indeed anyone else, and in disregard of my advice, met his Armenian friend and gone with him to Bethlehem. There he had made arrangements for buying the Dead Sea Scrolls.

I remember well the details of his story of this trip to Bethlehem. But in 1953, after my father's death, I was going through his papers and found an account of this episode in his private journal and will quote his own words:

I had planned to meet my Armenian friend again on November 28 and go with him to the Arab antiquities dealer. But my wife had been particularly adamant against my going, in view of the danger. And so I had reluctantly to call off the meeting. Later in the day, my son, Yigael, came in from Tel-Aviv and was as excited as I was when I told him of the scrolls. But he, too, indicated, though not as vehemently as his mother, that perhaps it was not too wise. He was only with me for a short while as he had to return to his headquarters in Tel-Aviv.

Later in the evening I listened to the radio and heard that the United Nations, which had been expected to vote on that day, had postponed its decision. Here I thought was my chance. For I believed that the Arab attacks would begin immediately after the vote, and if I were to go to Bethlehem it would have to be before. I therefore resolved to make the journey next morning, the 29th, and this time I decided not to tell anyone.

Next morning I telephoned my Armenian friend and told him I was coming over to see him right away. Armed with my pass I

21

entered Zone B once again and went straight to his store. I told him I was ready to go with him to Bethlehem.

We took the bus. I was the only Jewish occupant. The rest were Arabs. All of us felt the tension in the atmosphere. My friend told me later that he had really been scared stiff by the responsibility he had assumed by bringing me on that journey. But it passed without incident.

When we arrived in Bethlehem, we made straight for the attic of the Arab house in which the antiquities dealer, Feidi Salahi, lived. Among the Arabs it is considered bad form to plunge immediately into business, and so, restraining my crude European behaviour, I followed local custom and made polite queries about his health and the well-being of his family, while we sipped coffee. But I don't know how I managed to disguise my eagerness and impatience. I was on tenterhooks all the time.

Our polite exchanges lasted half an hour. It seemed more like a year; and then our business talk started. I was grateful to my Armenian friend for sparing me the delicate task of opening. He asked the Arab dealer to tell us the story of the Bedouin. I had already heard it but it was a good tale. He told us how these Bedouin had come to him with 'leather bundles'. They had been moving with their goats along the north-western shore of the Dead Sea. While searching for a stray goat, they had stumbled across an opening in the rocks overlooking the sea. It excited their curiosity. They threw stones into the cavern and were surprised to hear a strange sound, as if the stones had hit and broken a piece of pottery. But they were too busy with their flocks to investigate, and so they returned the following day. Crawling into the cave they found themselves in a narrow crevice. On the floor were eight earthenware jars, five on one side, three on the other. Several of these jars were still covered with upturned dishes. Inside the jars they found bundles of leather, some wrapped in linen. While groping inside the jars, they accidentally broke some. For several weeks they had wandered about with the bundles, showing them occasionally to friends in their tribe who had visited them in their tent. They then decided to come to Bethlehem, the commercial centre of the Bedouin from the Judaean desert, and see whether they could get some money for their find.[1]

[1] We learned later that some of the scrolls had been acquired by a Syrian

He then brought out two jars, in which the bundles had been found, which he offered for our inspection. They were of a shape unfamiliar to me. He then carefully produced the leather scrolls. My hands shook as I started to unwrap one of them. I read a few sentences. It was written in beautiful Biblical Hebrew. The language was like that of the Psalms, but the text was unknown to me. I looked and looked, and I suddenly had the feeling that I was privileged by destiny to gaze upon a Hebrew scroll which had not been read for more than two thousand years.

I examined the other leathers, while all the while I was wondering what to do next. I wanted to buy them and I wished to take them home with me then and there. But I had no serious amount of money with me and in any case it would take days to settle upon a price for such objects, for there is a special pattern to Arab bargaining, and a quick deal has no flavour. I therefore told the dealer that I was much interested, would probably wish to buy, but I should like to take them home with me for further scrutiny. I promised to let him know my decision, through our mutual Armenian friend, within two days. He agreed and wrapped the scrolls in paper. Tucking them under my arm we parted with friendly salaams.

Descending from the attic, my Armenian friend and I made our way to the Bethlehem market place where the Jerusalem bus was filling up. All around were groups of Arabs, some sullen and silent, others gesticulating wildly. I don't think it was imagination that made me sense a heightened tension in the atmosphere, but there was no incident. The package under my arm must have looked like a bundle of market produce. We entered the bus and reached Jerusalem safely. At the Jaffa Gate we got off and my companion let out a deep sigh of relief. As I bade him farewell, he exclaimed: '*Al-hamdulillahi*—thank God we have returned safely.' I left him and hurried home with my precious parcel.

I made straight for my study and unrolled the leathers. As I read the texts, I became more and more convinced that my first hunch had been correct and that I was witnessing a discovery of tremendous importance. I was enthralled by the beauty of the

Orthodox Christian antiquities dealer some time earlier, and that he sold them to the Syrian Metropolitan of the Monastery of St Mark in the Old City of Jerusalem.—Y.Y.

23

Hebrew. But the identity of the texts still eluded me. I looked up the Apocryphal books in my library to see if I could find parallels, but there were none. Here, then, were original texts. Nevertheless, unwilling to rely on my own judgement alone, I hastened out into the evening and called on several of my university colleagues who specialized in the Hebrew language and ancient literature. I asked if they had knowledge of these texts. They had not. I went home and sat reading the manuscripts. In the morning I had resolved to buy them, though it took another day before I was able to telephone my Armenian friend and instruct him to inform Feidi Salahi that I was buying the scrolls.

While I was examining these precious documents in my study, the late news on the radio announced that the United Nations would be voting on the resolution that night. My youngest son, Mati (who later became a pilot and was killed in action on a mission against an Egyptian warship during the War of Independence), was in the next room, twiddling radio knobs in an effort to get New York. He was tuned in to the United Nations and was following the speeches before the vote. From time to time he would give me a brief commentary on what had been said. It was past midnight when the voting was announced. And I was engrossed in a particularly absorbing passage in one of the scrolls when my son rushed in with the shout that the vote on the Jewish State had been carried. This great event in Jewish history was thus combined in my home in Jerusalem with another event, no less historic, the one political, the other cultural.

News of the United Nations' decision spread like wildfire through the city. Soon the streets were thronged with cars from which cheering youngsters were shouting the announcement to any who might have missed it on the radio. I could not remain indoors. I went out to share the joy with Jewish Jerusalem. Outside the building of the Jewish Agency there were massed throngs. I felt myself bursting with my own news. I had to tell someone about the great discovery. I searched for friends, and was delighted to spot two nearby among the crowd: Dr Yallon, the celebrated Hebrew grammarian, and Yitzhak Ben Yechezkiel, the writer and collector of Jewish folk tales. My news bubbled forth. I do not know whether they believed me or even whether they heard what I was saying, but in the turbulent emotional joy of that night, and sensing that I was transmitting something exciting, they responded with unrestrained delight.

A few days later, on my way to my lectures at the University on Mount Scopus, I met a friend who was an official in the University Library. I was still full of my news and told him about it. His eyes seemed to grow wider and wider as I told my tale, and then, to my astonishment, he capped it with a remarkable coincidence. A few months earlier, he said, the University Library had received a letter from Dr Magnes, the University President, telling them to send two of their officials to the Syrian Monastery of St Mark in the Old City to look at some manuscripts in the possession of the Metropolitan. He, together with another official, had been chosen to go. When they got there, the Metropolitan Mar Athanasius Samuel had told them that the manuscripts had been lying for a long time in the library of one of their monasteries near the Dead Sea. He wanted their opinion on their age and contents and on whether the University Library would be willing to buy them. They took the view that the scrolls did not seem to be very old, but suggested that the texts seemed to be Samaritan and advised that a specialist in Samaritan books be sent to examine them further. They had telephoned some weeks later to find out whether the Metropolitan still wished them to send the specialist, but he was away. And that's where the matter stood then.

All this had happened a few months earlier while I was on sabbatical leave in the United States. I was hearing about it for the first time. But as my friend spoke, it became clear to me that the scrolls that he had seen at the monastery were probably from the same batch as mine, and he had been told the story of their having lain a long time in a Dead Sea monastery library simply as a blind. I felt like rushing straight to St Mark's to examine the texts, but the entrance to the Old City was already blocked by Arab groups. However, if my theory was correct, I felt it important that any future negotiations, should they be reopened by the monks of St Mark's Monastery, should be handled on our side by me. I therefore went to Dr Magnes and received his authority.

A few days later I received a telephone call from the Armenian telling me that he hoped to get some more scrolls from the same source fairly soon. The problem of money began to worry me. I imagined I would have to pay several hundred pounds if many more scrolls became available and I wondered where I could lay my hands on such a sum. I went to my bank and asked for a personal loan of £1,500. Since I did not wish to embarrass the manager, who might respect my scholarship but not my financial status, I offered my small house in Rehavia as a mortgage. This he accepted and I was given the appropriate forms of sureties to sign.[1]

Meanwhile the security situation in Jerusalem became increasingly grave. Communication between the two communities in the country almost ceased. In Jerusalem, Arabs and Jews dared not enter each other's quarters. But ignorance of what was happening to the other scrolls gave me no rest. Despite the warnings of my Armenian friend, I several times went into his quarter to meet him and to urge him not to let the matter drop but to keep going to Bethlehem to prod the Arab dealer there to get whatever else he could from the Bedouin.

I had not read at that time the complete texts of the scrolls in my possession. I had read only those parts which unrolled with ease. The work of unrolling ancient manuscripts is delicate, for the danger of disintegration is high. It calls for specialist skills. Fortunately we found in Jerusalem among the Jewish refugees from Germany such a specialist, Dr J. Bieberkraut. As he worked and as we read each fragment which he unrolled we were astonished by the contents. Brought to light was an Apocalyptic work of unknown origin, in beautiful Biblical Hebrew, which told of a battle between the Sons of Light (the Jews) and the Sons of Darkness (the Edomites, Moabites, Syrians and other neighbouring peoples). Another scroll revealed chapters of Hebrew verse which read like Psalms.

One day towards the end of January 1948, I received a letter from the Arab quarter of Jerusalem. It had taken three days to come from the other side of the city. The letter was from an acquaintance of mine, a member of the Syrian Orthodox Christian Community, in whose grounds near Talpioth I had made, two years earlier, the discovery of an ancient Jewish tomb, dating from the first century AD. In his letter the Syrian wrote that he wished to

---

[1] Prospects later became brighter for the raising of the purchase price from public funds, and my father was accordingly persuaded by friends to discontinue his efforts to receive the personal loan.—Y.Y.

show me some ancient Hebrew scrolls which he had in his possession and wondered where we could meet. We decided on the YMCA building in Jerusalem. This was then in military Zone B. I equipped myself with the necessary pass.

At that time the YMCA building was much used as a meeting place for Arab leaders. In order not to arouse too much comment I packed several books under my arm and entered the YMCA as if I were about to change these volumes at the library. I saw many Arabs sitting on the terrace. They looked somewhat startled to see a Jew enter this building and they must have thought me a crazy bookworm to think of using the YMCA library at such a time. I was happy to spot my friend among the sitters. The YMCA librarian, who was also a Syrian Orthodox Christian, and who had been apprised of our meeting, saw me and ushered me into a private room. He asked me to wait a few moments: shortly afterwards my friend appeared. From a safe in the room the two of them produced several ancient scrolls which they put on the table. There to my great joy I saw a scroll containing what looked to me like the entire book of Isaiah.

I glanced at the other scrolls and it was clear to me that these were of the same origin as those I had myself obtained from the Bethlehem dealer. Within a few minutes the following fact had been established: my Syrian friend had really bought them from a Bedouin of the same Ta'amira tribe who had brought the other scrolls to the Bethlehem dealer. According to him these scrolls now belonged to the Syrian Metropolitan and to himself. He asked my opinion on their genuineness and I replied that I considered them to be old manuscripts. I added that I would be willing to buy them for the Hebrew University and I suggested that I should take them home for further examination. I also wished to show them to Dr Magnes, the president of the University. I promised to bring them back within a few days. He agreed to this proposal. I accordingly took the manuscripts with me and went home.

During the next few days I read what I could of the scrolls, and also showed them to Dr Magnes and to two of my university colleagues, who specialized in Biblical research. I returned to the manuscripts continually, day and night, sometimes even getting out of bed in the small hours of the morning to read them and to make copies of some of the texts. The Isaiah Scroll interested me particularly and I copied several of its chapters.

I was still unable to make up my mind about the price that should be offered to the Syrian. I was convinced however that this batch of scrolls would certainly be more expensive than the first. Moreover, knowing something of the mentality of oriental antiquities dealers, I was well aware that whatever I offered he would always think that he could get more from somebody else. How right he was! But I had the feeling that if I were not merely to offer, but actually lay on the table, two thousand pounds sterling, he would not be able to resist. But where was I to lay my hands on such a sum? I went again to my bank to ask for the loan but alas, the political and military situation was by then so grim that I was refused. How bitterly I now regretted that I had permitted myself to be dissuaded from raising that loan earlier. However, the money had to be found and I decided to ask the Jewish Agency for it.[1]

Unfortunately, its headquarters had shortly before been moved to Tel-Aviv, and communications between Jerusalem and Tel-Aviv were neither regular nor safe. I went to the Director of the Bialik Foundation, the literary institution of the Jewish Agency, to find out if he had any means of getting in touch with Tel-Aviv. He told me that Mr Isaac Gruenbaum, member of the Executive of the Jewish Agency and its representative on the Bialik Foundation, was in Jerusalem, and he offered to bring him to me the next day. This was the day when I promised I would return the scrolls to the Syrian at the YMCA. To my deep regret circumstances made it impossible for them to see me and I had to leave for my meeting at the YMCA without having contacted them.

It was Friday the 6th of February that I made my way again to Zone B with the precious scrolls in my hand. I feared that I might never see them again. In the YMCA the Syrian was waiting for me. Almost his first question was: 'How much do you offer?' I countered by asking him to name the price. Neither of us would name the figure and we finally arranged to meet the following week at the Yugoslav Consulate. He on his side would bring with him the Metropolitan and I would bring with me Dr Magnes, and we

---

[1] The Jewish Agency for Palestine was an unofficial precursor of the provisional Government of Israel.—Y.Y.

would try to reach agreement. I walked home slowly. The deserted streets fitted my mood of empty depression.

Shortly after my return the two members of the Bialik Foundation came to see me. Too late, alas, to see the borrowed scrolls. I showed them instead some fragments of the scrolls already in my possession and Mr Gruenbaum was so impressed that he promised to go the very next Sunday to Tel-Aviv to talk the matter over with Mr Ben-Gurion.[1]

A few days later he returned to Jerusalem and told me that the Jewish Agency leaders had been so impressed that they were willing to put at my disposal any sums I needed for the purchase of the scroll. Weeks passed but the promised letter from the Syrian, confirming the meeting at the Yugoslav consulate, did not arrive. Eventually I received a letter informing me that they had decided not to sell. They preferred to wait until the world was once again open to them, and they could find out the market price. I later discovered what had happened. Some two weeks after I returned the scrolls one of the Syrian priests had gone to the American School of Oriental Research and had met some of its members. The Americans had managed to obtain permission to photograph and publish the scrolls, assuring the priest that they would be able to get far higher prices for the scrolls in the United States.

Thus the Jewish people have lost a precious heritage.

So my father believed—a belief in which he died in 1953. He was not to know that the scrolls were to be restored to the Jewish people and permanently housed in Jerusalem, and that I, his son, in the strangest possible way, would have something to do with their acquisition.

This ends the saga of the first three scrolls and how they came into the possession of the Hebrew University. These scrolls are The War of the Sons of Light against the Sons of Darkness, The Thanksgiving Scroll and a scroll of the prophet Isaiah. (This is now known as 'Isaiah MS 2'; of one the four scrolls we acquired later was also a copy of Isaiah, which is now called 'Isaiah MS 1'.) It was my father's for-

[1] Mr. Ben-Gurion, Prime Minister of Israel, was at that time Chairman of the Executive of the Jewish Agency.

tune to see part of these scrolls published during his lifetime. In his diary I found the following words written on the 1st of December, 1947: 'I have read a little more of the leathers. I tremble as I think about them. This may be one of the greatest discoveries in the country—a discovery of which we could never have dreamt.' How right he was!

Let us now follow the journey of the other four scrolls.

The late Professor E. L. Sukenik, the author's father, studying a scroll

CHAPTER 2

The Monastery of St Mark

THE SECOND Bethlehem antiquities dealer who had bought scrolls from the Bedouin was a Syrian Orthodox Christian. In the early summer of 1947 he got in touch with a possible purchaser, the Syrian Metropolitan, Mar Athanasius Samuel, at the Monastery of St Mark in the Old City of Jerusalem. The Metropolitan, telling his side of the story later, said that when he first heard about the scrolls from the merchant in Bethlehem he immediately showed interest and decided to buy them, although he had not yet realized the extent of their antiquity. Some weeks passed before a meeting was arranged, and the dealer said that he would bring both the scrolls and the Bedouin who had found them. On the appointed day the Metropolitan waited all morning, but by noon, since they had not turned up, he went out to lunch. On his return to the Monastery, he was told by one of the monks that some men with 'dirty rolls' had called during his absence but since no one had known of the purpose of their visit, and since the rolls were written in Hebrew and not in Syriac, he had sent them away advising them to contact a Hebrew institution.

The Metropolitan, however, managed to contact the dealer once again and asked him to return to the Monastery with the Bedouin. This they did, and after relatively short negotiations he bought four complete scrolls from them. One of his immediate actions was to despatch some of his monks with the Bedouin to find the cave in which the scrolls had been discovered, in the hope that others might be found. The cave was just as it had been described by the Bedouin, but—according to the Metropolitan's story—because of the great heat, his

31

party could not search for long and returned empty-handed.

Thereafter, the Metropolitan sought the opinion of scholars and experts as to the value of the scrolls. He showed some of them to a high official of the Mandatory Government Antiquities Department, an Armenian, and to a member of the École Biblique (the French Dominican School for Archaeology and Biblical Study in Jerusalem), but neither realized their importance. In the absence of an encouraging opinion, he went—according to his story—to the Syrian Patriarch of Antioch. He too, gave it as his view that the scrolls were no more than three hundred years old, but he did advise the Metropolitan to consult a Professor of Hebrew at the American University of Beirut. The professor was away from Beirut at the time and the Metropolitan returned to Jerusalem with the scrolls. He then contacted—among others—two officials of the Hebrew University and the Jewish National Library, but they too failed to recognize the significance of the scrolls. These were obviously the two officials of whom my father had written.

Some months elapsed without any further action being taken by the Metropolitan. But we now know that his interest was revived when he heard from members of his congregation of the purchase made by my father, Professor Sukenik, and of his interest in the Metropolitan's scrolls. Moreover, as we have already seen, some of the scrolls had previously been on loan to Professor Sukenik, who returned them to the owners as he had promised. This occurred on the 6th of February 1948. Contrary to their promise the members of the Syrian Church did not return with the scrolls. What they did instead, it transpired later, was to take them for an opinion to the American School of Oriental Research in Jerusalem. This led to their first transatlantic journey.

For many years the American School of Oriental Research had served as the centre of archaeological studies in Palestine. Credit for this must go mainly to Professor W. F. Albright of Johns Hopkins University in Baltimore, who directed it for a number of years. At the beginning of 1948, the head of the School was Professor Millar Burrows of Yale, but in February he was on a visit to Iraq. His place in Jerusalem was taken temporarily by John C. Trever, one of the Fellows of the School. When Professor Burrows left on his trip and Professor Trever took over, neither could have foreseen what a dramatic month February was to prove.[1] On the afternoon of Wednesday, the 18th February, 1948, the School's cook called him to the telephone to speak with someone who had asked to be put in touch with the director of the School, in connection with some ancient Hebrew manuscripts. Father Butros Sowmy, a Priest of St Mark's Syrian Orthodox Convent, in the Old City of Jerusalem, was on the other end of the line. He told Trever that while he was tidying up the Convent's library he had stumbled on some scrolls in ancient Hebrew script, which were not mentioned in the catalogue, and he would like Trever's advice about them. Trever invited him to come to the School on the following day, and at two-thirty Father Butros arrived with his brother.

Opening their small leather suitcase, they took out the scrolls wrapped in newspapers, and a separate small fragment.

Carefully [writes Trever] they unwrapped one of the smaller ones, which has since proved to be a part of the Sectarian Document.[2] It was so brittle that they opened it only a little for me to see. Meanwhile Father Butros took out the largest one, calling my attention to it. Putting the first one down, I took the large one, and finding it much more pliable, laid it down on the bed and began slowly to unroll it. It was rolled with the end of the manuscript on the outside, and the last two columns, being on a single sheet of parchment, had become separated from the rest when the thread with which it had been sewn had disintegrated. The last column of writing covered only five-eighths of the available space and was badly worn from handling in ancient times. I unrolled about a dozen columns, peering intently for possible indications of authen-

[1] Trever's account of these events is given in *The Biblical Archaeologist*, Vol. XI, 1948, p. 46 ff. (The American Schools of Oriental Research, New Haven.)

[2] It was the Manual of Discipline.—Y.Y.

ticity, not yet sure that what I was seeing was not a forgery, though the scrolls had every appearance of great antiquity. Their script, though obviously Hebrew, looked strange to my inexperienced eyes.

Later Father Butros told Trever the truth about the discovery including the story of the Bedouin, the dealers in Bethlehem, and how the scrolls had reached the Metropolitan Athanasius. Trever describes his feelings after the priests had left the School:

Sleep was almost impossible that night. Numerous questions flooded my mind. How long was the large scroll? How much of Isaiah was there? Could it be authentic? Those few evidences of a corrector's hand on the last twelve columns seemed a certain argument for authenticity. But how could such a perfect manuscript be as old as the Nash Papyrus? Out of sheer exhaustion I fell asleep, still arguing with myself!

Despite the difficulties of reaching the Old City of Jerusalem, Trever managed to get through to see the Metropolitan himself on the following day. He begged to be allowed to photograph the manuscripts, but the Metropolitan refused.

Did they realize [wrote Trever] that by photographing them and getting them widely distributed, their monetary value would be greatly increased—witness the Codex Sinaiticus?[1] This argument seemed to appeal to them, for we began to consider how it was to be done. They finally accepted my invitation to bring the scrolls the next morning to the School, where all my equipment would be easily accessible.

Although Trever had used this argument at the time solely in order to secure permission to photograph, later events were to prove the validity of his reasoning. For several days Trever and his colleague Brownlee worked to photograph the four scrolls, and were even successful in sending a few photographs to the United States for Professor Albright's opinion.

[1] On this Codex see chapter 10.

On the 15th of March they heard from him by air mail: 'My heartiest congratulations on the greatest manuscript discovery of modern times . . . I should prefer a date around 100 BC. . . . What an absolutely incredible find! And there can happily not be the slightest doubt in the world about the genuineness of the manuscript.'

The political situation in Jerusalem, meanwhile, had deteriorated considerably. The Mandatory Government was about to leave the country, and fighting between Jews and Arabs had become more intense. Under these conditions the Americans considered it safer to take the scrolls to the United States. To quote Trever once again: 'On March 18th we invited the Metropolitan to visit the School for discussions. Dr Burrows presented him with a suggested news release, for his consideration and approval. For the first time then he was made aware of the real significance of his manuscripts. He was delighted.' A few days later, on March 26th, Trever was urgently called to the Metropolitan who 'informed me that Father Butros had left that morning with all the manuscripts, to take them to a place of safety outside Palestine. . . . This was the news we had hoped to hear for some days; *indeed, we had urged upon them the importance of the move*'.[1]

Word of the discovery was now officially out. Although it was known that the scrolls had been discovered in a cave near the Dead Sea, this was little help to scholars, who still knew nothing of its whereabouts; the conditions that prevailed in Palestine in those days made it difficult for scholars on different sides of the border to keep in touch with each other or to go in search of the cave.

When full-scale war broke out in the late spring of 1948, UN military observers were the only people who were allowed to cross from one side of the fighting front to the other. One of these observers, Captain Lippens, of the Belgian Army, had taken a particular interest in the scrolls. In his official capacity he was in touch with both sides and had

[1] Author's italics.

heard much from scholars in both countries. He resolved to secure help from the Jordanian authorities to try and search for the cave in which the scrolls had originally been found, which was in Jordan-controlled territory. Assisted by Arab Legion soldiers placed at his disposal, and after a three-day search at the end of January 1949, he found the cave. This started a series of systematic digs in the area.

First to follow Captain Lippens to the scene were Gerald Lankester Harding, Curator of Antiquities for the Jordanian Government, and Père de Vaux of the École Biblique et Archéologique Française, who headed an expedition which set out on 15th February to make a systematic excavation of the cave. From the very outset the excavators realized that they had been preceded by non-professional searchers, who had conducted some barbaric and illegal digging. This was later confirmed both by the Bedouin and by members of the Syrian Church in Jerusalem. Harding writes that the Bedouin, 'reported that during the next few months, people from the Monastery made frequent visits there, enlarging a lower entrance and excavating it very thoroughly. In the course of this work they must have recovered all the rest of the known manuscripts and large fragments'.

The Metropolitan's decision to take the scrolls to the United States is described by Harding in an even less diplomatic manner: 'Later he smuggled out of the country the Isaiah Scroll, the Manual of Discipline, the Habakkuk Commentary, the Lamech Apocalypse, some large fragments of Daniel, and eventually took them to USA with him.'

In January 1949, the Metropolitan arrived in the United States with the scrolls, at the invitation of Professor Burrows. Subsequently facsimiles of three out of the four scrolls were published by the American School of Oriental Research and edited by Burrows.

The events that followed, and how the Metropolitan tried in vain to sell the scrolls, were best described by Edmund Wilson in the *New Yorker* of May 1955, and later in his book

The Scrolls from the Dead Sea. He had an interview with the Metropolitan which was most significant in showing that despite the fact that the enormous value of the scrolls had been recognized by then, by a quirk of fate it was impossible for them to be sold at that time. Wilson writes:

The Metropolitan was hoping then to sell the scrolls to some institution of learning, but this had been more difficult than the Americans had led him to believe. The publication of the texts by the School did not have the effect that had been predicted of exciting an interest in buying the manuscripts; on the contrary, it diminished their market value. Since the texts were available to scholars, there was no need to have the manuscripts in their libraries. . . . Dr Burrows of the Yale Divinity School has been active in connexion with the scrolls, and the Library of Yale University at one time considered acquiring the manuscripts, but finally decided not to. Those interested in the scrolls have complained—not without a certain justified bitterness—that the Library has had no difficulty in raising a sum that has been quoted at four hundred and fifty thousand dollars in order to buy the Boswell papers but could not produce the probably smaller sum that would have bought what are, without any question, the most precious discoveries of their kind since the texts of the Greek and Latin classics brought to light in the Renaissance. This was all the more unfortunate because everything had not yet been published. There was a group of fragments of Daniel, that the Metropolitan had not released, as well as a whole manuscript that had not even been read. . . .[1]

In the meantime, the scrolls were not sold, and the scholars were becoming impatient and worrying for fear the manuscripts might be deteriorating. The Metropolitan, when he brought them to the United States, had put them in a safe-deposit vault, and he had made them the charge of a trust, the trustees of which were Syrians of the Metropolitan's own Church. All business connected with them was to be transacted in the name of the trust, the proceeds from selling them were to be handled by it, and the money was to be devoted to church work and education. By this time, the Metropolitan had announced that he would not sell the Lamech

[1] The so-called Lamech Scroll.

roll separately. Since the value of the other manuscripts had fallen with their publication, he would now have less chance of disposing of them without the inducement of the unread scroll. He had decided to sell them in a lot, but not to set a definite price on them. He offered to have them appraised by experts. That he should have had to wait in vain for an American buyer throws into relief the false values of the market for rare books in this country. One remembers the one hundred and fifty thousand dollars paid by Dr Rosenbach for a copy of the Bay Psalm Book, the one hundred and six thousand paid by him for a Gutenberg Bible, the fifty thousand for the first version of *Alice in Wonderland*. The difficulties about the Metropolitan's title may possibly have had something to do with the reluctance of learned institutions, but undoubtedly the principal obstacles were the relative poverty of such institutions—divinity schools and seminaries—as are interested in Biblical manuscripts and the high susceptibility of rich collectors, cultivated by the book dealers through decades, to first editions of classics that are perfectly accessible to everybody.

Mr Bieberkraut unrolls the Genesis Apocryphon Scroll

CHAPTER 3

Destiny

In 1953 I was in England, engaged in archaeological research. Since the publication of the three scrolls in possession of the Hebrew University had not been completed by my father before his death, I had been requested by the University to help in preparing the book for publication. At the same time I was asked to prepare, as a separate work, a comprehensive commentary on one of the manuscripts, the scroll of the War of the Sons of Light against the Sons of Darkness. This was dear to my heart, partly because of its fascinating military aspects and also because I had managed to peruse rather more of this than the other two scrolls during my father's lifetime. I accordingly interrupted my previous research and spent more than a year in the examination of and research on that particular scroll. In May 1954 I was invited to visit the United States on a lecture tour. I hesitated long before replying—I had been working rather hard to complete the two books for the University Press, and travel would be tiring—but in the end I accepted the invitation. I could hardly have guessed what this decision was to mean to me and my country.

It did not occur to me to investigate the whereabouts of the four scrolls which were taken to America by the Metropolitan as I had not heard of their adventures. I was vaguely aware that they had not yet been sold, but this I ascribed to what I had heard was the high price demanded by the Metropolitan. Exaggerated reports had reached me that he was asking for several million dollars.

On Thursday, 27th May 1954, I was invited by Professor William F. Albright to lecture at the Johns Hopkins University on the Dead Sea Scrolls in possession of the Hebrew

University. After the lecture, while chatting informally with Albright, I asked him why the Americans had not yet published the fourth scroll. To my surprise he said that the Metropolitan refused to allow its publication unless all four scrolls were bought from him. 'Why don't the Americans buy the scrolls?' I asked. 'Surely a few million dollars for such a purpose is not too difficult to raise.' Professor Albright's reply astonished me even more. He told me that there was no talk of a few million dollars—the sum involved was probably in the region of half a million dollars. He added that for various reasons, including those later mentioned by Wilson in his articles and book, it was impossible to find an institution or an individual willing to buy the scrolls. Remembering my father's suffering during his last few years because he had been unsuccessful in purchasing the scrolls for the Hebrew University, I asked Professor Albright: 'If this is so, why don't I try to buy them for Israel?' He replied that as far as he knew the Metropolitan was desperately seeking a buyer and since he could not find one in America, he saw no reason why I should not try. He promised to find me the Metropolitan's address, though I said I was afraid that if I approached him directly, agents from one or two Arab states might intervene and prevent him from selling to Israel. The Jordanian Government had already declared him a smuggler and a traitor, and this would lay him open to further trouble.

After that talk I turned to more lectures in New York and other cities, but the thought of the scrolls was continually in my mind. Could they be bought? Could *I* buy them? And where could I find the money?

A few days later, on the first of June, I received a telephone call out of the blue. The voice identified its owner as Monty Jacobs, a young man I had known from his service days in Israel. He was now on a journalistic assignment in the United States. He was sorry to trouble me, he said, but had I by chance seen the *Wall Street Journal* that day? I thought he was joking, for he knew I wasn't interested in stocks or shares.

40

He explained that the paper had published a small advertisement about the Dead Sea Scrolls. Having read a report on my Johns Hopkins lecture on the subject, he thought I might be able to explain the advertisement, in which there might be a story. I asked him to come to my hotel at once with the paper. He arrived a few minutes later and together we turned to page 14. There, among scores of other commercial and business advertisements, was a small two inch by two inch paragraph which read:

> '*The Four Dead Sea Scrolls*'
>
> Biblical Manuscripts dating back to at least 200 BC are for sale. This would be an ideal gift to an educational or religious Institution by an individual or group. Box F. 206 *The Wall St. Journal.*

I read and re-read the advertisement. It was almost incredible, and yet it seemed to fit the story Professor Albright had told of the Metropolitan's difficulties. He might have turned to the advertising columns of the press as a last resort. The more I read the more convinced I became that these were the scrolls that the Syrian Christian had promised to bring to my father in Jerusalem in February 1948. I was resolved to do everything possible to acquire them. I told Jacobs that I hoped to find out more about them, that I believed them to be the genuine article, and would do my utmost to secure them, but that caution and secrecy were essential. I therefore asked him to keep the information to himself, promising that if anything resulted from my efforts, he would be the first reporter to hear about it. He was sitting on a possible scoop, but he had to keep sitting. In the days that followed, he telephoned me daily to find out if there were any developments. But his eagerness could not match mine.

At first I hardly knew what to do. A direct approach to the advertiser might endanger the whole purchase. I decided to find a reliable man, who was familiar with business procedure, but who would not be immediately associated with Israel. I consulted a relative of my wife, Mr T. Bennahum, a businessman from New York. I told him the story and he showed immediate enthusiasm. On his advice we decided to proceed with the deal in the customary manner for the purchase of *objets d'art*. He would arrange for a banker friend to write to the box number and request further details. Next day, the 2nd of June, the following letter was despatched by the banker:

Box F. 206, *The Wall Street Journal*,
44 Broad Street,
N.Y.4, N.Y.
Gentlemen,
   On behalf of one of our customers, I am writing you for additional information regarding the 4 DSS. which you advertised in yesterday's *Wall Street Journal*. My customer is anxious to have further details regarding these scrolls at an early opportunity. If you will please contact the undersigned, I will make the necessary arrangements to have a representative examine the scrolls and with whom you may negotiate.
                                    Yours very truly,

A few days went by and there was no reply. Although lectures and journeying about the country kept me very busy, I still found time to think long and often about the scrolls. Why was there no reply? Had someone else got in ahead of me? I confess that on the lecture platform during those days I may well have startled my audiences by a wandering mind. Five days later the banker received a reply. It was dated 4th June and read:

   Received your letter in reference to the 4 DSS and wish to thank you for your interest in this matter. I am enclosing a brief description and history of these scrolls which may be of some use to your client. I shall be glad to make an appointment for negotiations and for proper examination of these scrolls, provided your client already has some knowledge about them. Will you please inform me if your client has some realization of their historical value and worth or shall it be advisable for me to send you more references regarding these documents.

Yours very truly,

Charles Manoog

Trustee for 4 DSS

There was no end to our delight. We asked our go-between to telephone Mr Manoog and confirm the receipt of his letter. He followed it up with the following note:

Dear Mr Manoog,

In accordance with our telephone conversation of this morning, this is to acknowledge and thank you for your letter of June 4th regarding the 4 DSS. If you will be so kind as to let me know when you expect to be in N.Y., on Thursday or Friday, I will set up an appointment for you to meet my client's representative.

Awaiting your early reply, I am, etc.

Our next step was to arrange a meeting for the preliminary discussions. At this meeting Manoog indicated that the price of the scrolls was rather high and as an example he said that the Isaiah Scroll alone was insured for a sum well over $400,000.

On Friday, 11th June, after lengthy negotiations, Mr Manoog agreed on behalf of the Metropolitan to sell the four Dead Sea Scrolls for $250,000. It was agreed that if the customer for whom the banker was acting consented to the price, Manoog would see to it that the contract of sale was properly set out with the Metropolitan himself, who at that time was staying in Florida.

When Theo Bennahum rang me to tell me the results of the meeting I felt for the first time that our object was really within reach. My second thought was a question. Where would I lay my hands on a quarter of a million dollars? Until that moment the problem had not seriously come up. Theo and I had vaguely mused over the question, flinging at each other stray suggestions of wealthy acquaintances who might finance the purchase, but now that the problem was immediate and urgent, we recognized that it would not be easy to find the funds at such short notice. We approached some people who showed interest and who promised to think the matter over. But it was clear that the thinking process would be long and protracted. I finally decided that the moment had arrived when I should inform my government, and request it to lay out the money or at least guarantee a loan until the complete sum was collected later. I accordingly hurried over to our Consul-General in New York, Mr Abe Harman, and told him the whole story. Harman was immediately infected by my enthusiasm, and together with Bennahum we sat down to discuss the situation. On Harman's advice we called in Mr Izhak Norman, director of the American Fund for Israel Institutions, and asked for his assistance. Mr Norman, however, could not make any definite decision without consulting his board, since such an enterprise was not directly within the range of the Fund's activities. On the other hand he happened to have at that moment in cash a considerable sum of the Fund's money, which he was willing to loan for a very short period if the Fund's board of directors consented. This consent was quickly secured, owing largely to the generous understanding of one of the largest contributors to the Fund and its present chairman, Mr Sam Rubin of New York. They agreed to loan us a considerable amount of the required price.

That afternoon I sent the following cable to Mr T. Kollek, Director-General of the Prime Minister's office in Jerusalem:

An unexpected miracle has happened. The four Dead Sea Scrolls, including Isaiah, brought to US by the Syrian Metropolitan, are offered for sale. They can be bought at once for 250,000 dollars. No need to stress the importance of the scrolls and the unrepeatable opportunity. Any delay may ruin our chance. Have already probed several important donors, and consider it certain that the sum may be collected within a year. A guarantee from the Treasury for the whole sum is imperative. Request your immediate action with the PM and Minister of Finance. Harman, who is near me, doing his best to help. I rely on you and expect a positive answer. Secrecy imperative. Yigael.

Two days later I received his reply:

The Prime Minister and Minister of Finance are delighted with the wonderful opportunity. Orders for suitable guarantee have been dispatched. *Mazel-tov!* Teddy.

An appropriate answer from a Prime Minister in the land of the Bible; but our financial troubles did not end there. Abe Harman and others still had to run about among various people to find the remaining cash, even as a loan. Still the guarantee from Jerusalem finally enabled us to overcome all obstacles.

On the 15th of June, in the early afternoon, our go-between informed us that he had definitely settled with Manoog on the sum of two hundred and fifty thousand dollars and if the sale deed were signed, we could have the scrolls. The next few days were spent with lawyers who worded the text of the contract to be signed by both parties. On the 18th of June Manoog informed our banker friend that the Metropolitan had confirmed the transaction, but that the completion of the deal would have to be postponed for a few days, for he wished to sign the contract himself and bring the scrolls with him. But since he was at that time in Florida and disliked air travel, it would take him several days to reach New York. We were reluctant to delay, for each day increased the dangers of a leakage of identity and intervention by the Arab States. But there was no alternative. We just had to wait patiently for the Metropolitan's arrival.

Meanwhile, Theo Bennahum had to leave for Europe on urgent business, and since we did not consider it wise for me to deal directly with his banker friend, we decided that Theo's business associate, Mr S. Estridge, should take over from him and sign the contract on our behalf. Mr Estridge was taken into our confidence, with no previous knowledge whatsoever of the problems and difficulties involved. But he grasped the complicated details immediately and displayed understanding, initiative and tact in his handling of the affair.

The days passed without word from Manoog. Finally when we got in touch with him he was unable to give us the date of the Metropolitan's arrival. We became worried, fearing some last minute hitch, but on the 28th of June, we had a message to say that the Metropolitan, Manoog and their lawyer would meet us at our appointed place with the scrolls on the 30th of June.

On the 28th of June I was scheduled to lecture to the America-Israel Society at the Library of Congress in Washington, on 'New Light on the Dead Sea Scrolls'. When I had agreed to give that lecture, a long time before, I had naturally no inkling that in the meantime I would be involved in the actual purchase of the scrolls for Israel. I felt rather uncomfortable when after that lecture some of my audience approached me to inquire as to the whereabouts of the four scrolls and what was being done with them. I fear my replies were somewhat evasive.

As the date of the meeting with the Metropolitan drew near, excitement mounted not only in New York, but also in Jerusalem. On the 30th of June I received a cable from Teddy Kollek containing just one word: 'Well?!'

That same evening Manoog rang up our go-between and asked him to postpone the meeting once more since the scrolls had not yet been taken out of the vault. Meanwhile our lawyers raised the legally logical question of whether anybody had examined the scrolls offered for sale to make sure they were the real ones and not fakes. Although I had no doubts on that score, the lawyers seemed justified in raising this point, and so the difficulty of finding a suitable person for their examination arose. For obvious reasons I could not go myself. I got in touch with my friend and colleague at the Hebrew University, Dr Kutscher, who was in New York at that time, and who was also engaged in scroll research. I could not tell him what it was all about on the telephone, but said that I might require his assistance in some urgent matter the following day. I asked him not to leave the city. He consented. When I then received information that the meeting with the Metropolitan had been postponed once more, I rang up Kutscher to ask him to remain in New York on the following day too. Unfortunately he had a previous lecture engagement elsewhere which he could not cancel. As I could not explain the urgency of the matter to him on the phone, I did not feel justified in pressing him.

Next day, the Metropolitan, Manoog and their lawyer finally arrived in New York and booked rooms at the Waldorf-Astoria. On the 1st of July, exactly one month after the advertisement in the *Wall Street Journal*, we embarked on the final stage of our negotiations. At one o'clock Estridge rang us to say that they were reaching the end of the transaction and completing the final wording of the contract and supplements, and that whoever was going to examine the scrolls should get ready to do so.

The situation was almost desperate, when I suddenly remembered my friend Professor Harry Orlinsky, who was also engaged in scroll research. I telephoned him and asked him to come and see me at once on an urgent matter. He told me that he was just about to leave for Canada on holiday, that his family were already waiting downstairs in the car for him and that he had just come back for the last suitcase when he had heard the telephone bell. I impressed on him the extreme urgency of the matter and assured him that he would not regret the rearrangement of his plans. It was also necessary to convince his wife and they both agreed. When he arrived and I told him the story, he almost collapsed with excitement and relief. On his way to me, he had imagined all sorts of reasons for my call, but this was not one of them. There was no time to lose. I handed him Professor Burrows' two-volume facsimile of the scrolls and asked him to check each page. It was agreed that he should introduce himself as Mr Green, an expert on behalf of the client. He left.

A little while later he rang back to say that he had checked the scrolls, found them in excellent order, except for one page from the Commentary on Habakkuk which was missing. The Metropolitan assured him that the page must have been left in the vault by mistake and promised to send it to him at once. We therefore ordered Mr Estridge to complete the sale without further delay, and not wait until the missing page was sent. In the meanwhile the lawyers on both sides found some minor technicalities which they wanted to look into, and the final meeting was again postponed until the following day.

Professor Orlinsky, having completed his task, returned and wrote the following statement:

Dear Mr Yadin,

This is to inform you that I examined this afternoon the 4 DSS which formed the subject of negotiations between Mr Sydney Estridge and the representatives of the Archbishop Samuel of the Syrian Church, Jerusalem. I made a detailed inspection of the scrolls and compared them with the official reproduction published by the American School of Oriental Research, New Haven, edited by Professor Millar Burrows. I am satisfied that the scrolls, which formed the subject of the above negotiations, are the authentic 4 DSS referred to and reproduced in the a/m work by Professor Burrows and that they are complete. There is one reservation to the above, to which I immediately drew the attention of Mr S. M. Estridge, namely that the right hand fragment of the first page of the Habakkuk Commentary reproduced on Pl. 55 (columns 1, and 2a) of the Millar-Burrows volume I is missing. The 4th Scroll, so called Lamekh scroll, is still unrolled. There are two fragments of it separately.

Harry M. Orlinsky

As for that missing page, the Metropolitan did keep his word and a few days later the page reached us by registered mail. It is of interest in this connexion to note Trever's words when he first examined the Habakkuk Scroll in Jerusalem:

> He [the Metropolitan] took me into his office and handed me a folded sheet of paper. Within the folds was a piece of one of the scrolls! Instantly I recognized it as a portion of the Habakkuk Scroll; for the colour of the leather on which it was written, the script, the size and the shape all coincided. The edges were eaten away by worms, as was the beginning of that scroll, and it looked exactly like the missing right-hand part of the first column, the absence of which had been such a disappointment to Dr Brownlee when he was studying it.

Next morning, all formalities having been completed, we were finally informed that the scrolls were in the Waldorf-Astoria vault, and now at our disposal. Our excitement was indescribable. Estridge, my wife, and I went there in one car, followed by a van in which to load the precious purchase. The scrolls were packed in a large black trunk, and the porters who helped us put it in the van must have thought it was full of treasure. They were right, but they could never have guessed the nature of the treasure. At eleven-thirty we had the trunk safely stored away.

I decided that the seal on the trunk should be broken at the Israeli Consulate in the presence of Monty Jacobs, the newspaperman who first called my attention to the advertisement, who for a whole month had kept his promise of silence. While waiting for him to arrive, Abe Harman and I sent a cable to our Government. The press that morning had been full of rather worrying news from Israel, with reports of unrest along the border, and clashes between Israel settlers and Arab saboteurs. We knew that the Prime Minister and his colleagues must be preoccupied by this situation, and we worded our cable as follows:

> To Teddy Kollek, for the Prime Minister, Minister of Finance and President of the Hebrew University. For the difficulties that are now facing you, find consolation! The treasures of the past are in our hands as from this morning at 10.30. Will send them to Jerusalem next week. Writing in detail.

The Premier's reply was characteristic: 'My enthusiastic congratulations on your achievement.'

At one forty-five Monty Jacobs arrived and in a shuttered room of the consulate in the heart of Manhattan, we opened the big black trunk with three scrolls, and a small wooden box containing the fourth unrolled scroll. We then drank *Lechaim*, the Hebrew toast, which means 'To life'.

There was no end to our delight. The three scrolls of Isaiah, Habakkuk and the Manual of Discipline were all there and complete. They were most beautifully preserved and separately laid out in transparent perspex boxes. It must be said in commendation of the Metropolitan that he had kept them perfectly. The fourth scroll, the Lamech Scroll, as it was then called, had not yet been unrolled and was kept like a delicate baby in a small wooden box padded with cotton wool. It was in a very fragile state and we refrained from handling it too much, despite the itch in our fingers.

We now had two more problems: to find the money and repay the loan, and to get the scrolls safely to Israel. We got in touch with several leaders of the Jewish community, in the hope of finding among them, or through them, some person wealthy enough and interested enough to purchase these scrolls for Israel. Mrs Rebecca Shulman, the Hadassah leader, after some meditation, mentioned the name of Mr Samuel Gottesman, New York industrialist and benefactor: he was, she said, generally interested in cultural activities, and he might quite possibly be attracted by these unique objects and this unique purpose. Mrs Shulman introduced us to his sister-in-law, Mrs Esther Gottesman, herself a Hadassah leader. She was excited by our story, transmitted it with enthusiasm to Mr Gottesman and arranged for me to meet him. I showed him the scrolls, explained their significance and value, and proposed that he should make a gift of them to the State of Israel. He was interested, but naturally could not commit himself on the spot since the sum involved was so large.

Actually, considering the British Government's payment of

a hundred thousand pounds in 1933 for the Greek Codex Sinaiticus, dating back to the fourth century AD, the price of the Dead Sea Scrolls did not seem unduly large. I told this to Mr Gottesman, showing him the official communiqué issued by the British Museum.

In addition I showed Mr Gottesman parts of a letter which I had received a few days before from Professor Albright, after I had telephoned him about buying the scrolls, and told him of the price we had paid. Professor Albright wrote:

In my opinion the price you mentioned over the telephone is a bargain. . . . Quite aside from the unique value of the three principal scrolls in the St Mark's lot, is the importance of the book of Lamekh which has not yet been unrolled but will provide a fairly lengthy text in Jewish Aramaic during the last two centuries of the second Temple. Its importance for the history of Biblical Jewish religious literature is also very great. I should not consider a price of half a million as at all excessive for a lot of manuscripts of this unique importance. Fifty years ago it would certainly have been priced in the millions, but income tax and other developments have changed all that.

Next day I lunched with Mr Gottesman and his son-in-law, on which occasion the former told me that he was willing to contribute the major part of the money required. Thus the main problem found a partial solution. As for the dispatch of the scrolls to Israel, we arranged for each scroll to be sent separately.

On the following day I left the United States for England by sea, having pre-arranged with Abe Harman a code which would advise me of the arrival in Israel of each scroll. Each was given a Hebrew name. My days on the boat were accordingly made pleasant by the receipt of such cables as: 'Simcha leaving today'—Simcha being the Manual of Discipline—followed by 'Simcha arrived safely'; followed in turn by 'Chaim leaving today' and 'Chaim arrived'. By the time I reached London, the whole of my 'family' had arrived in Israel.

The Government of Israel decided to mark the acquisition of the scrolls by establishing in Jerusalem a special Shrine of the Book, to house these priceless manuscripts. At a meeting of the Israeli Cabinet a Shrine of the Book Trust was appointed, with the President of the State as its permanent head. One of the trustees appointed by the cabinet was Mr Samuel Gottesman.[1]

Until these technical formalities and most of the financial arrangements were completed, the Government was not anxious to announce the acquisition of the scrolls. By early February 1955, all was ready and on the 13th of that month Mr Moshe Sharett, then Prime Minister of Israel, called a special press conference of representatives of the world and local press, and told them the story. While he was speaking, I, in London, received the following cable from Teddy Kollek: 'At this memorable moment the Prime Minister is telling the country and the world about the homecoming of the scrolls. Excitement and joy are great.'

He was right. In the Israeli newspapers next day, all world and other local news was relegated to second place. The front pages and editorial columns were filled with the story of the scrolls.

One month later, at a special ceremony at the Israel Embassy in Washington, in the presence of the Diplomatic Corps and distinguished scholars, the manuscripts were formally named the Gottesman Scrolls.

Thus ended the adventures of the seven Dead Sea Scrolls, from the moment of their chance discovery by the Bedouin on the shores of the Dead Sea until their return to their home in Jerusalem. There, in the Shrine of the Book which is about to be built, they will be the most prized exhibits in what is intended as a centre for Biblical and scroll research for scholars all over the world.

[1] It was only after the completion of this manuscript that I learned with deep regret of the death in New York of Mr Gottesman. His place as trustee of the Shrine of the Book has been taken by a member of his family.

PART II

CHAPTER 4

The Cave of the Scrolls

RESEARCH into the origin and meaning of the Dead Sea Scrolls began almost as soon as they were brought to light, and continues to this day.

Archaeology laid the indispensable groundwork. In February 1949, as we have seen, Gerald Lankester Harding and Father R. de Vaux led the first proper investigation of the cave in which the scrolls had rested for two millennia.

Despite the ransacking of the cave by the Bedouin, and thanks to the expert work put in by the expedition, many important facts were accumulated. They first discovered that the cave was an entirely natural cleft in the rock, originally entered by a small hole fairly high in the wall. Later excavations suggest that there may have been a lower entrance which collapsed long ago but this is not certain.

The first action of the archaeologists was to re-examine the heap of earth piled close to the cave by the illegal diggers. This re-examination uncovered many pottery sherds of the type of the jars in which the scrolls had been found; some fragments of torn cloth similar to those in which the scrolls had been wrapped; and even a few pieces of inscribed leather, among them one—until then the only one—in ancient Hebrew script and not in the square Hebrew script with which the other scrolls were written.

The excavations inside the cave revealed hundreds of minute pieces of scroll and also some scraps of papyrus. Among the special finds worth mentioning were some remnants of phylactery cases, lamps, and, of course, sherds of pottery jars of various types, all similar to the jars which had housed the scrolls.

The cloth wrappers, only parts of which were discovered, deserve a more detailed description. From the thorough investigation conducted by Mrs G. M. Crowfoot many interesting facts were brought to light about their nature, quality, design, appearance and method of weave. The cloth was linen.

On the whole the spinning is fairly good, but it varies, and sometimes the yarn is loose and has a woolly appearance but this may be due to deterioration; the warp is usually rather harder and more even than the weft. Though the thread is never very fine the linen is of fair quality. The highest counts recorded are 18×18 per cm and 20×16 per cm, while the lowest is 10×8 per cm. The weavers seem to have been aiming at an even 'linen weave' and occasionally achieved it. . . . On other cloths sometimes there are more wefts than warps and sometimes warps predominate.

Not everywhere was it possible to reconstruct the measurements, as they obviously varied. A number of the wrappers were of a particular design which invariably had blue linen lines. The dye used was probably indigo. As for the design itself, Mrs Crowfoot writes:

The usual form it takes seems to be simple blue lines in the weft, generally of two wefts only; in one case the wefts are double and in one there is an embroidered line added. The only attempt at a more elaborate pattern is . . . a design of rectangles within each other.

From Mishnaic sources we know that it was customary to wrap the holy books in cloth kerchiefs, some of which bore designs. The Mishnaic tractate *Kil'ayim* refers in chapter 9, verse 3, to '. . . wrappers for scrolls (of the law)' as not being subject 'to the law of Diverse Kinds. But R. Eliezer forbids them [if they have in them wool and linen].' In chapter 28, verse 4 of the Mishna, tractate *Kelim*, there is mention of cloth wrappers of scrolls in the record of a controversy between the two major schools of Talmudic thought:

Scroll wrappers, whether figures are portrayed on them or not, are susceptible to uncleanness. This is the view of the School of Shammai. The School of Hillel say: if figures are portrayed on them they are not susceptible to uncleanness; if figures are not portrayed on them they are susceptible. Rabban Gamaliel says: in either case they are not susceptible to uncleanness.

These sources show that it was customary to make kerchiefs with a design on them, but we know nothing of the details of that design. The significance of the design on the Qumran kerchiefs is similarly not easy to fathom. But there must have been some meaning to it to justify the highly complicated and difficult weave. Mrs Crowfoot writes:

The decoration is simple enough, but on examination presents a most intriguing weaving problem, for the blue weft threads actually turn round corners and become warps. This was at first very difficult to prove, but can be clearly seen in enlarged photographs and drawings. . . . My own view is that these lines were woven, but it has been suggested, in view of the obvious difficulties, that embroidery, in a kind of drawn thread-work, would be easiest. We have in several other examples lines in the weft which are obviously woven, and one of embroidery, a darned line between two woven ones, so both weaving and embroidery are in use for the blue decoration on these cloths.

This leads us to conclude, with Mrs Crowfoot, that the design in question of interlocked oblongs had a definite significance, otherwise they would not have gone to the trouble of copying out so complex a process. Mrs Crowfoot may be correct in assuming that the design signifies a building or shrine that was holy to the sect. We shall have to await further discoveries before reaching a final solution.

These cloth wrappers of the scrolls, which helped greatly in their preservation, were of major importance in establishing the age of the scrolls. Some of these cloths were sent to Professor W. F. Libby of Chicago University for a Carbon 14 test. This is a test whereby it is possible to establish the age when organic matter ceased to live. It is accurate to within four hundred years, that is plus or minus two hundred years of the date established by the test. It is therefore an important aid to archaeologists in confirming the approximate era of their finds and in exposing modern fakes. The scroll wrappers were submitted to this test since their component, linen flax, was an organic body about which Carbon 14 could provide information. The result of the test put its date at AD 33, so that the age of the wrappers could have been as early as 167 BC or as late as AD 233. As we shall see later, the results of the excavations and of the contents of the scrolls lead us to put the general date that they were copied either at the first century BC or the early part of the first century AD.

The cliffs of the caves

CHAPTER 5

The Other Caves

ALTHOUGH it may have been natural to assume that the first cave would not be the only one, and that others were to be found in the same neighbourhood, the scholars did not begin to look for them until after another cave had been found, once again by the Bedouin of the Ta'amira tribe. It seems to be the fact that most of the important cave discoveries then and later were made by these Bedouin who would come forward to do their searching as soon as the scientific expedition had left the area. The Bedouin, with their desert experience, discerning eyes and limitless amount of time, were more capable of catching glimpses of rocky crevices and clefts that were likely to be of interest, than the scholars who could only stay in the area for short periods due to lack of means and trying conditions.

And so, in February 1952, when the expedition was busy searching the caves that had previously been discovered in Wadi Murabba'at, south of Qumran,[1] they heard that the Bedouin had discovered another cave, close to the first Qumran cave, and had found in it fragments of scrolls. This prompted the scholars to proceed on a systematic survey of the whole cliff from north to south, and uncover all its caves. An expedition thus set out on March 10th of that year and worked until the 29th. The cliff was searched for a stretch of eight kilometres from a place called Hajar el Assad in the north to a point one kilometre south of Ras Feshkha. Some thirty-seven caves were investigated and in twenty-five of them pottery sherds were found, identical with the type of jar discovered in Qumran 1. Fragments of cloth, similar to

[1] This is described more fully in Chapter 8.

those already described, were also found. But scraps of scrolls were found in two caves only: the one discovered by the Bedouin and now known as Qumran 2, and another now called Qumran 3. Qumran 2 seemed to have been considerably looted on previous visits by Bedouin, but the scholars succeeded in finding a few scroll fragments and several sherds of pottery, like the ones in Qumran 1. The leather fragments belonged to many Biblical books such as Jeremiah, Exodus, Leviticus, Numbers, Deuteronomy, Ruth, and Psalms. Among non-Biblical books was a Hebrew fragment from the book of Jubilees. Altogether, the non-Biblical books were represented in some forty fragments of scrolls.

The excavators seemed to be luckier in Qumran 3, about two kilometres north of Qumran 2. The cave's ceiling must have collapsed in ancient times and broken the jars, and this exposed the scrolls to rats and humidity, causing them great damage. Nevertheless many small fragments were discovered, the most interesting containing the beginning of Isaiah. But the greatest surprise was found near the entrance of the cave. It was the discovery of two copper scrolls, one on top of the other. The contents of these scrolls are so interesting and startling that a separate chapter will be devoted to them later in the book.

As long as the scholars were busy around the caves, the Bedouin kept away and refrained from independent digs. But as soon as the scholars left, the Bedouin immediately swarmed over the area, and once again it was their lot to discover the most interesting finds. This time they discovered a new cave, now referred to as Qumran 6, in which were fragments of an older copy of the famous Damascus Covenant found many years ago in the Cairo Genizah, which will be discussed later. Still more important was their discovery of a hewn chamber, not in the cliff but on the plateau between the cliffs and the sea, not far from Khirbet Qumran. That chamber, now known as Qumran 4, yielded more fragments of scrolls than were found anywhere else, and it caused the members of the expedition to return to the site in September 1952, when they found another cave, now known as Qumran 5. For once this was a cave not previously discovered by the Bedouin and thus all its treasures were intact and gave the scholars a good harvest. The contents included parts of the Book of Tobias, pieces of phylacteries and some Biblical fragments dealing with the 'End of the Days'. Qumran 4 yielded fragments of no less than sixty manuscripts of books of the Bible, including Genesis, Exodus, Leviticus, Numbers, Isaiah, Deuteronomy, Psalms, Daniel, Jeremiah, and most interesting of all, some fragments from Samuel with a text that is quite different from the traditional Hebrew Masoretic text, but similar to the text of the ancient Greek translation, the Septuagint.

But in none of the caves and in none of the discoveries so far known to the world, have any complete manuscripts been found. So far, the seven scrolls in Jerusalem are the only complete Dead Sea texts to have been discovered. It is our hope that they will not remain so, and that future excavations will uncover new intact scrolls.

Many of the discoveries have not yet been published and we shall have to wait patiently until we can appreciate these treasures. Still, in spite of the extraordinary significance of these cave discoveries and despite the obvious implication that this was the library of a sect that inhabited the caves, nothing was known of their way of life and their spiritual centre, and even certain archaeological data about the time of the scrolls was lacking. The answer to these questions was found in later excavations not far from the caves themselves.

CHAPTER 6

The Communal Building or Khirbet Qumran

THE DISCOVERY of the caves containing the scrolls raised the immediate question of whether the people who had hidden the scrolls had also lived in the vicinity, or whether they had come from afar especially to hide their treasures in this desolate region. The answer, which was greatly to help our understanding of the character of the sect concerned, was found in the next excavations. We pointed out earlier that the cliffs in which the caves are located do not rise directly above the sea. They start about one mile west of the sea and continue in a south-easterly direction for some three and a half miles, touching the sea at a place called Ras Feshkha, south of Ain Feshkha (the spring of Feshkha). Between the cliffs and the sea there is a plateau, split by wadis. On top of the plateau, some four hundred to five hundred metres east of the caves, there were some ancient ruins long known by the Arabs as Khirbet Qumran. These ruins are north of a wadi called Wadi Qumran. The character of the ruins and their size had many years before established them as the remains of a Roman fort of the first few centuries AD, rather than the dwelling place of a large indigenous community. The distinguished French scholar, Clermont Ganneau, who visited the site at the end of the nineteenth century, wrote:

The ruins are insignificant in themselves; they consist of a few dilapidated walls of low stones and a little cistern (*Birkeh*) with steps leading down to it. The soil is scattered with numerous pot sherds of all kinds. If a town, in the full sense of the word, ever existed here, it must have been a very small one.

60

After de Vaux and Harding had started excavations in the caves of Qumran, they decided to excavate the ruin too, in the hope of finding some link between it and the caves. Those excavations, which were begun at the end of 1951, not only answered the question as to whether people had actually inhabited the neighbourhood, but yielded much new information. As a result we now know that people did in fact live and die in the area; that they dwelt in tents and booths of which nothing is left and that the ruins contain the remains of the central building which served as a sort of community centre. The particular size and lay-out of that building, and the finds which were discovered there, enable us to reconstruct in some measure their way of life and the structure of their society.

A description, even brief, of the building itself and the various periods in which it existed, of the scientifically conducted excavations and of the hundreds of coins found on the site, throws light on the history of the sect and its period, and automatically provides information about the scrolls.

The Khirbeh consists mainly of the remains of one large, rectangular building measuring thirty by thirty-seven metres. It was apparent that the building had been in use several times at separate periods. The general lay-out of the building in the first period, i.e. the earliest, was as follows: in its north-western part, there was a large square tower of about ten by ten metres and with very thick walls of 1·3 metres. The tower had two floors. At the bottom there were several intercommunicating rooms, without external windows, which served, in the opinion of the excavators, as storerooms. The placing of the tower at the north-western part of the building suggests that it was meant to serve as a defence against attacks coming from either Jericho or Jerusalem. The top floor of the tower had three rooms or large halls, one of which was particularly long, measuring four by thirteen metres. The other two were smaller and measured eight by four metres each. This group of rooms must have served for the communal activities of the people in the neighbourhood; a theory supported by what was found in them.

To the east of this group was a large courtyard. Running off its northern corner was another room, some four by ten metres, which, from all the evidence, seems to have served as the communal kitchen or cookhouse. Running off the north-east corner of the kitchen was another square hall similar to the tower and divided into several rooms, from which there was an exit leading out of the building. South of the central yard a number of smaller rooms were discovered, the use of which has not yet been established, but in one of these a number of small basins were found. There was also one complete jar with the name of its owner inscribed on top: *Yohanan Ha-taleh*, i.e. John the Young.

The south-east corner of the building consisted of an independent block, separated from the other rooms. This block contained two beautifully built and plastered pools, a small square one measuring two by two metres, and a larger oblong one measuring three by eight metres. To reach the latter, one had to descend some fourteen steps which are preserved to this day. To the east of the pools were several workshops, where some iron tools were found. Not far off was some sort of a privy.

The structure can thus be visualized as a communal building of comparatively large proportions with four main elements: a fortress with a corner tower; a group of halls that must have served as prayer-rooms, dining-rooms or writing-rooms; the water pools and a group of service rooms like the cookhouse and workshops. In the excavations carried out in April 1955, a mill and a baking oven were discovered outside the building. This division is confirmed by the finds discovered during the excavations.

The building was abandoned for the first time due to serious damage suffered from an earthquake, signs of which are still visible, fortunately, in the tower and in the pools.

The earthquake, which must have been catastrophic to the inhabitants of the building, enables a date to be set on its destruction and establishes the date of its rebuilding for the second time. In de Vaux's opinion the earthquake was probably the one mentioned and described in detail by Josephus in *Antiquities of the Jews*, Book 15, Chapter 5:

At this time it was that the fight happened at Actium, between Octavius Caesar and Antony, in the seventh year of the reign of Herod: and then it was also that there was an earthquake in Judaea, such a one as had not happened at any other time and which earthquake brought a great destruction upon the cattle in that country. About ten thousand men also perished by the fall of houses; but the army, which lodged in the field, received no damage by this sad accident.

The earthquake, therefore, took place perhaps in the spring of the year 31 BC, and that year saw also the end of the first community centre in Khirbet Qumran. Between two floors in a room adjacent to the main building a big hoard was discovered of about five hundred and fifty silver coins, the latest of which was struck in the year 8–9 BC. The coins were *above* the floor belonging to the phase of the building destroyed by the earthquake, but *below* the floor of the subsequent building, and were apparently stored away by the occupants of the latter. For many years thereafter the place must have been deserted, to judge from the almost complete lack of Herodian coins. But after a while it was repaired and re-inhabited, to begin its second period. The lower parts of the outer walls were encircled by supporting walls, forming a kind of revetment four metres high. Minor alterations were also made in the interior of the building. One of the two large rooms in the south-west corner was sub-divided by a wall, and in the other room a sort of bench was constructed running along all four walls. In the central yard a new room was added and the pools abandoned. Instead they must have used a large pool outside the walls of the building, which was visible on the surface even before the excavations were started.

It seems evident that these alterations were comparatively minor and did not change the public character of the building. On the contrary, some of the changes, like the addition of the bench in one room and the remains of a large oven in another, tend to confirm that the building did in fact continue to be used communally, its rooms serving as meeting or dining-rooms for the people of the sect. Among the most important finds were a large table, some five metres long and half a metre high, made of plastered clay, and the ruins of two shorter tables. It is possible, of course, that these served as dining tables. But de Vaux also discovered two ink pots, one of bronze and one of clay, of the type most common in the Roman period. The conclusion therefore seems natural that these tables were not dining but writing tables for the hundreds of books that seem to have belonged to the sect. The large room may not have been a dining-room but a scriptorium, or writing-room. The evidence is clear that this building too, like its predecessor, was destroyed. This time it did not fall into ruin with the passing of time, but was destroyed by war. There is proof of this in the layer of ashes. Dates of coins found in this stratum make it certain that its destruction occurred during the great revolt against the Romans between AD 66–70. This destruction saw the end of the communal building in Khirbet Qumran and of its inhabitants.

In its third period, the building did not serve in its previous capacities, but was in fact turned into a military camp. This is established by the decisive alterations in its structure. The tower was still in use, but all the large halls were subdivided into small rooms, thus bringing to an end their function as centres of communal activity. It is of interest that the northern wall was doubled in thickness. But the whole south-easterly corner of the building, on the other hand, was completely abandoned, as is seen from the division of the walls and the destruction of the strata. It is not only the architectural alterations that indicate the changed function of the building. The many arrow-heads and coins bearing the insignia of the Roman Tenth Legion show that, after the building had been destroyed for the second time, it must have been re-occupied at some later period by Roman troops. It is difficult to ascertain the length of time it was thus occupied, but it seems that the Roman soldiers inhabited it until about the end of the first century AD. Nor were the Roman soldiers the final inhabitants of the building. Although no further major structural alterations were carried out, other coins were found of the period of the Second Jewish Revolt (the Bar-Kochbah Revolt), suggesting that during the years AD 132–135 it was occupied by rebels. However, definite and precise information on this subject is still lacking.

The building then, in its two earlier stages, most probably served as a centre for the public activities of the sect which lived in the vicinity of the Dead Sea, and whose people occupied huts or tents around it. Proofs are the large halls, the scriptorium, workshops, cookhouse, and pottery. During these two periods the place was occupied by a sect that called itself, as we discover from the seven scrolls, the Sons of Light. In its third stage it was occupied by Roman soldiers, termed by the members of the sect the Sons of Darkness. What fate befell the sect after the destruction of the building is unknown. What is known is that they managed to hide their precious scrolls from the Sons of Darkness in the neighbouring caves.

The significance of these discoveries is not only in the fact that they reveal to us the way of life of the sect while it inhabited the area. They also prove the connexion between the scrolls and the building in which were found thousands of pottery sherds of the type that held the scrolls. Had additional proof been required of the antiquity of the scrolls, this fact would provide it.

CHAPTER 7

The Cemetery

FROM the preceding facts about the building and the scrolls,
it might be argued that the members of the sect may not have
inhabited the area, but only convened there occasionally. Or
maybe only some of them actually lived there. However, the
discovery of a cemetery near by, on the same plateau as the
Khirḅeh, south-east of it, is decisive evidence that the sect did
in fact live there. More than a thousand graves were counted
in the cemetery, tidily arranged in rows. Clermont Ganneau,
who had already conducted small excavations there at the end
of the last century, wrote:

The most interesting feature of Qumran, is the tombs which,
to the number of a thousand or so, cover the main plateau and the
adjacent mounds. Judging merely by their outward appearance
you would take them to be ordinary Arab tombs composed of a
small oblong tumulus, with its sides straight and its ends rounded
off, surrounded by a row of unhewn stones, with one of larger size
standing upright at either end. They are clearly distinguished,
however, from the modern Mussulman graves by their orientation
—a longer axis in every case pointing north and south and not
east and west. This very unusual circumstance, had already been
noticed by the Mussulman guides . . . who made the same remark
as our man, that these were tombs of Kuffar, that is to say unbe-
lievers, non-Mussulmans. I made up my mind to have one of them
opened . . . After having gone down about a metre, our workman
came upon a layer of bricks of unbaked clay, measuring $15\frac{3}{4}''$ $\times$
$8'' \times 4\frac{3}{4}''$ and resting on a sort of ledge formed in the soil itself.
On removing these bricks we found in the grave pottery that had
covered the half-decayed bones of the body that had been buried
there . . . There was nothing else whatever to afford any indication. The head was towards the south, the feet towards the north.

The cemetery of the Qumran sect

. . . It is hard to form an opinion as to the origin of these graves, chiefly on account of their unusual orientation. They may very well have belonged to some pagan Arab tribe of the period which the Mussulman called Jâhilîyeh, that is to say before the time of Mahomet. Indeed, if they had been Christian tombs they would probably have exhibited some characteristic mark or emblem of religious nature. The use of unbaked bricks to cover and protect the bodies; the considerable depth of the cavities, the regularity that pervades the arrangement and so on, show that these graves were constructed with a certain amount of care and with evident respect for their intended occupants.

The excavations conducted in the cemetery by de Vaux and Harding in recent years have completely confirmed the description given by Clermont Ganneau. Only now we know what was unknown to Clermont Ganneau: the cemetery belonged neither to Arabs of the Jâhilîyeh period nor to Christians. It belonged to the fascinating Sect of the Caves.

CHAPTER 8

Wadi Murabba'at or the Archives of Bar-Kochbah

WE HAVE seen how the Bedouin in the Dead Sea area, as a result of the world interest in the first discovery of the scrolls and the subsequent traffic of excavators, seem to have turned themselves from a tribe of shepherds into a tribe of amateur archaeologists. Towards the end of 1951, these Bedouin stumbled over a discovery which, had it been made earlier, or had it been the only find in the Dead Sea area, would have excited the scholarly world almost as much as the discovery of the scrolls. This was the find at Wadi Murabba'at, which adds greatly to our knowledge of the history of the second Jewish Revolt against the Romans. This is known as the Bar-Kochbah Revolt. Since this discovery was made simultaneously with the finds at Qumran, it lost some of its drama and the world today knows less of its significance than it should. There is even a tendency to confuse the two discoveries, and it may therefore be useful to add a word on Wadi Murabba'at; the discoveries there throw additional light on the finds in Qumran, and prove beyond doubt that, even after the destruction of the main building of the Dead Sea sect at the end of the first Jewish revolt, the Judaean desert continued to serve as an asylum for victims of persecution and for rebels. We have already seen that the Qumran building itself, sometimes in its third phase, served perhaps as a shelter or as some kind of habitation for people who were in revolt against Roman authority.

At the end of 1951, ancient documents differing from those found in Qumran began to appear on the antiquities market.

It was immediately obvious from their script that they were of slightly later origin than the manuscripts in Qumran. Harding and de Vaux, the directors of excavations in Qumran, at once made inquiries among the Bedouin as to the source of the new finds. It was no easy task. The Bedouin both refused and feared to tell the truth. Only after lengthy efforts did some of them consent to turn informer and take the scholars to the site of the new discoveries. To everyone's surprise, they were led to a deserted place on the western shores of the Dead Sea: about seventeen kilometres south and eight kilometres west of Qumran, and about three kilometres from the Sea, into a very steep wadi known as Wadi Murabba'at. This is how Harding describes it:

The Wadi Murabba'at or Darajeh, as it is called indiscriminately, is a great gorge, some two hundred metres deep, almost sheer on its north side, steeply sloping on the south. As it nears the Dead Sea the sides become completely vertical . . . The nearest point to which transport can be brought is the Beqei'e plain, three hours' walking distance from the caves. After rains the plain is impassable to cars and a seven hours' walk was involved either to Bethlehem or Nebbi Moussa. There is no cultivation or permanent settlement of any kind in the district, and the Ta'amira Bedou move their camps about, following the pastures. Fortunately there had been good rains before we got there, and while we were there, so there was a plentiful supply of water in the wadi bed. The Bedou depend mainly on the Roman cisterns, of which there are many on the track to the caves. Our supplies had to be maintained by mule, which met the car twice a week except when it rained. But even the mules could not make the final descent into the wadi loaded and everything had to be carried down the last stretch by the workers.

From this description of the site it seems evident that the rebels against the Romans who selected those caves in the wadi for their home did so deliberately. A site as deserted and as almost inaccessible as this would present a natural barrier against an advancing regular army.

When the excavators first arrived at the wadi, they saw a large number of Bedouin fleeing in great haste, having been surprised in the act of carrying out illegal digs. The scholars found four caves, two of them quite large, about fifty metres in length, five metres wide and five metres high. One of these, now known as Cave 2, is the more important. They also discovered subterranean passages. A superficial examination of the caves proved at once that this was indeed the source of the flood of documents appearing on the market. The expedition decided on the spot that a thorough excavation was necessary, and this was started in January 1952. The results were astonishing. It was quickly established that these caves had been in use not only in Roman times, but thousands of years earlier. Remains were found of the Chalcolithic Age, that is, the transition era between the Stone and Copper Ages, about the fourth millennium B C. They also found remains of the Early Bronze Age (about the middle of the third millennium B C), the Middle Bronze Age (the era of the Hebrew Patriarchs, in the middle of the second millennium), and even of the Iron Age (about the eighth and seventh centuries B C, the era of the Kings of Judah). However, of most interest to us is the discovery there of papyri and parchment. These were found mainly in Cave 2. The first group of finds were fragments of books of the Bible. Unlike those found in Qumran, all these were identical with the traditional text. The script, too, was different from the script of the Qumran scrolls, and is definitely of a later date. Biblical books represented in the fragments include Genesis, Exodus, Leviticus, and Isaiah.

The second important find was a complete phylactery. It consisted of a bag containing a thin band of rolled parchment inscribed with the following three Biblical passages: Exodus xiii. 1–16; Deuteronomy xi. 13–21; and Deuteronomy vi. 4–9. This last passage, which appeared on the extreme right of the leather, is the celebrated prayer called the *Shema*, which begins in English translation, 'Hear, O Israel, the Lord our God, the Lord is one.'

The third group of finds includes miscellaneous documents. One, for example, is a document in Greek which seems to be a marriage contract dated the seventh year of the reign of Hadrian, i.e. AD 124.

The fourth group of finds is the most interesting, since it contains original documents concerning the Bar-Kochbah Revolt itself. We know that this revolt occurred in the years AD 132–135 against the Romans, but we know very little else about it. All we had had before were coins struck at that period by the leader of the revolt, and there were occasional and fragmentary mentions of it in both Jewish and Christian writings. But there were such lacunae in the decisive and important chapters of this history that scholars even argued over the real name of the leader of the revolt, either Bar-Kochbah or Bar-Kozebah. Some claimed that his true name was Bar-Kochbah, which means Son of a Star, and that Bar-Kozebah, which could mean Deceiver, was the derogatory name given to him when the revolt failed. Others claimed the contrary: that his true name was Bar-Kozebah and that Rabbi Akiba who supported and backed him, and in fact thought that he heralded the beginning of the Messianic era, named him Bar-Kochbah, and applied to him the saying 'there shall come a star out of Jacob'. Any finds which could shed light on the revolt were therefore of great importance. In some of the Murabba'at documents we find his full title. The following is an important example: 'Year one of the deliverance of Israel by Simon son of Kosebah, Prince [or President] of Israel.'

One of the documents found was an order written by the leader himself to one of his commanders whose centre had been Wadi Murabba'at. This order (like the other document), bears out the view of those who thought that Bar-Kochbah was the name given to him by Rabbi Akiba. It is worth quoting, though some of its details are not quite clear. It runs:

From Simon Ben Kosebah to Yeshu'a Ben Galgola and soldiers of the fortress, greetings [literally: peace]. I take heaven to witness against me: mobilize from the Galileans whom I have saved [or whom you have saved] everyone; for [otherwise] I shall put irons on your feet as I did to Ben-Aphlul.

Simon Ben Kosebah, Prince of Israel

This letter shows us that Simon Ben Kosebah was in the habit of issuing direct and short orders to his sub-commanders; that he demanded absolute discipline; and that he was ruthless towards those who disobeyed him. The word 'Galileans' too, is interesting. Who were they? Were they, as some scholars tend to think, Christians, or were they members of a Galilean sect that lived in the neighbourhood of Khirbet Qumran itself? We cannot yet give a final answer. Scholars are also arguing over the word 'mobilize'. The word in the original Hebrew is: וּפְקֹד Some prefer to read it וּפְסַד or וּפְסַק in the sense of 'perish', which would render the reading 'let every man perish with the exception of the Galileans whom I have saved'. I personally prefer the first rendering, 'mobilize'.

Another document of interest is also addressed to the same Yeshu'a Ben Galgola, who is here described as Head of the Camp, i.e. Commander of the Army, and is written by several leaders of the community in a village called Beth Mashkho. In their letter these leaders complain that a cow, belonging to Ya'aqov ben Yehuda, citizen of Beth Mashkho, was carried off by someone named Yehossef ben Ariston. There is a pathetic explanation of why they had to put the complaint in writing instead of coming in person before the commander, 'because the gentiles [Romans] are approaching us', or 'are in our vicinity'.

The documents from the archives of Yeshu'a Ben Galgola, leader of the revolt in the Dead Sea area, form a unique treasure. It is indeed, the only original archive known from the period of the end of the Second Temple and the revolt.

PART III

CHAPTER 9

The Scrolls: General

BEFORE we proceed to a description of the scrolls and their contents, let us deal with two questions which are being asked by the interested layman: is this the first time in history that scrolls have been found in jars in caves, especially in that neighbourhood? How were the scrolls written and on what material?

The custom of hiding scrolls in jars in order to preserve them for a long time is known even in the Bible. Jeremiah (xxxii. 13 ff.) says, for example:

And I charged Baruch before them, saying: Thus saith the Lord of Hosts, the God of Israel: Take these evidences, this evidence of the purchase, both which is sealed and this evidence which is open; and put them in an earthen vessel, that they may continue many days.

There is an interesting description of the process of preserving scrolls by sealing in jars in one of the pseudepigraphical books, *The Assumption of Moses*. Chapter i, verse 17 has the following passage:

And receive thou this writing that thou mayst know how to preserve the books which I shall deliver unto thee: and thou shalt set these in order and anoint them with oil of cedar and put them away in earthen vessels in the place which He made from the beginning of the creation of the world, that His name should be called upon until the day of repentance, in the visitation wherewith the Lord will visit them in the consummation of the end of the days.

This quotation is interesting since it is possible that this book was written by a member of the Dead Sea sect.

In the Talmud, we find the following: 'The Scroll of the Law that faded, should be hidden with a scholar. . . . Rav Aha the son of Jacob said: and in an earthen vessel.'

Most areas of Palestine are humid and thus unsuitable for the preservation of scrolls. It is therefore natural that the only place in which scrolls were indeed found—and possibly the only place in which any scrolls are likely to be discovered in the future—is the neighbourhood of the Dead Sea, the driest region of the country. Have scrolls ever been found there in the past? What little information we have of early discoveries of scrolls in Palestine shows them to have been found in the areas of the Dead Sea and Jericho.

The earliest and most interesting knowledge we have of this subject concerns Origen, who lived from AD 185–254. Origen was mainly known for his great work on textual criticism, the *Hexapla*, and the story comes from two sources: from Origen himself and from Eusebius in his well-known *Ecclesiastical History*. This is what Eusebius writes:

And so accurate was the examination that Origen brought to bear upon divine books, that he even made a thorough study of the Hebrew tongue, and got into his own possession the original writings in the actual Hebrew characters, which were extant among the Jews. Thus, too, he traced the editions of the other translators of the sacred writings besides the Seventy [the Septuagint] and discovered certain others differing from the beaten track of translation, that of Aquila and Symmachus and Theodotion, which, after lying hidden for a long time, he traced and brought to light, I know not from what recesses. With regard to these, on account of their obscurity (not knowing whose in the world they were) he merely indicated this: that the one he found at Nicopolis near Actium, and the other in such other place. On the other hand, in the Hexapla of the Psalms, after the four well-known editions, he placed beside them not only a fifth but also a sixth and seventh translation; and in the case of one of these he has indicated again that it was found *at Jericho in a jar* in the time of Antoninus the son of Severus.[1] All these he brought together,

[1] i.e., the Emperor Caracalla, AD 211–17.

dividing them into clauses and placing them one against the other, together with the actual Hebrew text: and so he has left us the copies of the Hexapla, as it is called.[1]

Origen's own words were as follows:

. . . the fifth edition which I found in Nicopolis near Actium. The marginal notes in it show how far (another similar text) differs from it. The sixth edition which was found together with other *Hebrew and Greek books in a jar near Jericho* in the time of the reign of Antoninus (MS. Antonius) the son of Severus. . . .[2]

It is of course difficult to tell whether this means that the scrolls were actually found in the Qumran caves themselves, but the fact that the discovery of earthen jars was made near the Dead Sea, at such an early date, strengthens the assumption that they may well have been found in these same caves.

Equally sensational information, though of a later date, is contained in the letter of Timotheus I, Patriarch of Seleucia (AD 726–819) to Sergius, Metropolitan of Elam (died about 805). This letter, which was first brought to the notice of scholars by Professor Eissfeldt, is written in Syriac.

We have learnt [writes Timotheus] from trustworthy Jews who were then being instructed as catechumens in the Christian religion *that some books were found ten years ago in a rock dwelling near Jericho*. The story was that the dog of an Arab out hunting, while in pursuit of game, went into a cave and did not come out again; its owner went in after it and found a chamber, in which there were many books, in the rock. The hunter went off to Jerusalem and told his story to the Jews, who came out in great numbers and found books of the Old Testament and others in the Hebrew script; and since there was a scholar well-read in literature among them, I asked him about many passages which are quoted in our New Testament (as) from the Old Testament but are not found anywhere in it, neither (in copies found) amongst the Jews nor (in those found) amongst Christians. He said (that) they are

---

[1] *Ecclesiastical History*, VI, 16; quoted in Paul E. Kahle, *The Cairo Geniza* (London, 1947), p. 161.

[2] Quoted in Kahle, *The Cairo Geniza*, p. 161.

there and can be found in the books discovered there. When I heard this from the catechumen and had also interrogated the others without him and heard the same story without variations, I wrote about it to the eminent Gabriel and also to Šubḥālmāran, Metropolitan of Damascus, (asking them) to search those books and see whether the passage (saying) 'He shall be called a Nazarene' . . . and other passages quoted in the New Testament as from the Old Testament but not found in the text which we have could be discovered anywhere in the Prophets. I also asked him if the following words, namely. 'Have pity upon me, God, according to Thy mercy . . . sprinkle me with the hyssop of the blood of Thy cross and cleanse me', should be found in those books, without fail translate them for me. This expression does not appear in the Septuagint nor in those other (translations) nor in the Hebrew (text). But that Hebrew said to me: 'We have found more than two hundred Psalms of David among our books.' I wrote to them about this. I thought nevertheless that these books had been deposited [in the cave] by the prophet Jeremiah or Baruch or by some other of those who had heard the word of God and been moved by it; when indeed the prophet learnt by divine revelation of the conquest, plundering and burning, that was to come upon the people for their sins, they then hid and secreted the scriptures (in holes) in rocks and caves, being firmly convinced that nothing of the word of God falls to the ground, in order that they might not be burnt in the fire nor carried off by plunderers; those, however, who hid them died in the course of seventy years or before that and, when the people returned from Babylon, there was no one left of those who had deposited the books (in the cave) . . . . If these passages occur in the books named, they are clearly more trustworthy than those (in use) amongst the Hebrews and amongst us. I have received, however, no answer to my letter from them on these points, and I have no suitable person whom I can send. This is as fire in my heart, burning and blazing in my bones.[1]

Timotheus' letter, though much later than Origen, shows that even at the end of the eighth century many manuscripts of the kind found in 1947 and later were discovered near the

---

[1] Quoted from G. R. Driver, *The Hebrew Scrolls* (Oxford, 1951).

Dead Sea, perhaps even in the same caves. The parallel of the events that led to the discovery is amusing—in the eighth century the hunter's dog, in the twentieth century the Bedouin's goat. Most significant of course is Timotheus' news that many of the manuscripts reached the Jews of that period. They must therefore greatly have influenced their writings from the ninth century onwards. One of the books probably discovered at that time, was the 'Covenant of Damascus', a copy of which was later found in the Cairo Geniza. This fact made some scholars believe, when the 1947 scrolls were discovered, that they too belonged to the Middle Ages, owing to the similarity between them and some books of the Middle Ages. But now we know that that similarity is due to the direct influence of the earlier discovered scrolls on the literature of the day.

A third item of information on this subject comes to us from the famous Karaite—that is, heretical Jewish—commentator Qirqisani, writing in the ninth century, not long after Timotheus. In one of his books on the different religious sects in old Judaism, Qirqisani refers, *inter alia*, to a certain sect which he called 'the sect of the Cave, because their books were found in a cave'. Qirqisani notes, incidentally, that this sect was different from other sects in that it had a separate calendar and its books dealt, among other subjects, with exegesis and discussion of the Bible. Significantly enough these two characteristics are typical of what we now know, from the scrolls, of the Dead Sea sect; it is almost certain that this was the sect to which Qirqisani was referring. It is equally certain that the books found in the cave were in fact the books mentioned a few years earlier by Timotheus as having reached the Jews of Jerusalem.

Among these three notes from the past, two indicate clearly that the discovery was made around Jericho, and the third and latest, without specific mention of the location, helps, by describing the contents, to establish the scrolls as similar to those found in the Dead Sea area, and the cave as almost certainly in that region. It is not surprising, therefore, that in the latest excavations many of the caves, as we have seen, were found to be empty of scrolls, despite the presence of many sherds of jars. There was clearly looting of those caves not only in 1947; it had started at least some seventeen hundred years earlier.

On the second question, about the material of the scrolls and how they were written: the scrolls are all of animal hide and are written on the *hairy* side of the leather, which was specially treated. Leather is known to have been used for inscription in the ancient East for a long time. Frederick Kenyon writes:

Coming nearer to the Greek world we have the statement of Herodotus (v. 58) that the Ionians had from antiquity called books *diphtherai* (Greek for leathers) because once, when papyrus was scarce they had made use of goat-skins and sheepskins. He adds that even in his own time many barbarous peoples used skins as writing materials. No doubt he would have included under this head the peoples of Syria and Palestine, where we know leather to have been regularly used. The Talmud required all copies of the law to be written on skins, and in roll form. . . . In this the Talmudists were no doubt only confirming the existing and traditional practice; and such evidence as exists tends to support this view.[1]

As a matter of fact the Jews continued using leather for their books long after the classical world had started the use of papyrus and parchment. An interesting paragraph on the use of leather for the holy scriptures in the centuries before the destruction of the Temple is found in the famous letter of Aristeas, who lived in the third century BC in Alexandria. In a letter attributed to him, he describes how the Greek Septuagint translation of the Bible originated:

When they entered with the gifts which had been sent with them, and the valuable skins, on which the law was inscribed in

[1] *Books and Readers in Ancient Greece and Rome* (Oxford, 1932), pp. 42–3.

gold in Jewish characters, for the skin was wonderfully prepared and the connexion between the sheets had been so effected as to be invisible, the king as soon as he saw them began to ask them about the books. And when they had taken the rolls out of their coverings and unfolded the pages, the king stood still for a long time; and then making obeisance about seven times, he said: 'I thank you my friends, and I thank him that sent you still more, and most of all God, whose oracles these are.' (176–7)

In accordance with the customs of the period or the specific rules in Talmudic literature, the writers of the scrolls used to rule the page horizontally with faint parallel lines with the aid of a hard stylus. The letters were 'hung' from those lines, that is to say the tops of the letters touched the top line rather than, as is our custom today, the bottom of the letter touching the lower line. Vertical lines were used to separate the pages from each other. Each writing sheet had several pages and the sheets were sewn together with dried tendons or flax threads. The writers left margins at the top and bottom of the pages, and a margin between the pages themselves. Following the custom of the day they did not use punctuation, but chapters were clearly marked by the leaving of a space, one or two lines wide, between the end of one and beginning of another. Most of the writers seem to have been experts and to have mastered the art of calligraphy. They used ink-wells, some of which, as we have seen, were found in one of the chambers of Khirbet Qumran. Despite their care it was inevitable that errors in writing should occur, and the number of these varies with the different scrolls. The system of correcting mistakes varied in accordance with the prevalent custom of the period and the rules preserved in Talmudic literature. If the writer had omitted a word or a letter, he would usually insert it above the line in the suitable place. If he had written superfluous words or letters, he would sometimes, instead of erasing, put dots either above or below the unwanted script. If the writer decided on erasure, he would, if the letter he wanted was similar in form to the one to be removed, erase only part of it, and re-write it to the form of the letter required. If the writer started a wrong word and realized it before its completion, he simply left it unfinished, and after leaving a little space began afresh.

These corrections often produce a natural source of discussion and controversy among scholars. It can be imagined that many tend to ascribe significance to letters which are simply words started incorrectly by the scribe and left uncompleted. On the other hand it is only after grave consideration and study that a scholar will dismiss a baffling letter or word, which eludes his understanding, as the lapse of an errant scribe.

The entrance to Cave 4

CHAPTER 10

The Isaiah Scrolls

A word about Bible texts in general, both in Hebrew and in translation, may be useful before plunging into the description of the Isaiah scrolls in our possession, and of their significance for Biblical research. Strange as it seems, the earliest known Masoretic (i.e. traditional Hebrew) text in existence, according to Kahle, dates back only to the year AD 895. Kahle says in this connexion:

the oldest dated Masoretic text of the Hebrew Bible preserved to us [is] the Ben Asher Codex of the Prophets in the Synagogue of the karaites in Cairo (A.D. 895) [p. 108]. . . . The other codex is the MS of the whole Bible, preserved in the Synagogue of the Sephardic Jews in Aleppo [p. 57].

The Aleppo codex dates back to about AD 929. Moshe ben Asher, who copied the earlier Cairo codex, is certain to have devoted all his ability, diligence and energy to finding the most accurate text amongst the sources at his disposal. He records that he wrote the codex in Tiberias and adds this on the colophon of the codex:

As it was understood by the congregation of the Prophets, the chosen of the Lord, the Saints of our God, who understood all the hidden things and embellished the secrets of wisdom, the chiefs of righteousness, the men of faith. They have not concealed anything of what was given to them, and they have not added a word to what was transmitted to them, and they have strengthened and made mighty the Scriptures, the Twenty-four Books, and they have established them in their integrity with explanatory accents, with a commentary of pronunciation with sweet palate and beauty of speech.[1]

[1] Kahle's translation, p. 111.

81

We see, therefore, that although the people of the Masorah (literally, 'Tradition') endeavoured to hand over as accurate a text as was possible and based their work on earlier manuscripts, we were not in possession of full texts of the Bible in Hebrew earlier than the end of the ninth and beginning of the tenth centuries. As for translations of the Bible into other languages, and especially into Greek, the earliest known translation, is of course, the Septuagint, which is believed to have been made at the end of the third century B C. Professor Orlinsky, one of today's world authorities on the subject, writes:

It is not unlikely that even before the Septuagint translation came into being, some individual attempts were made by Alexandrian Jews, translating part of the Torah into Greek. This was done in the same spirit that several English translations of parts of the Bible were made by Christians in England before the so-called King James Version was done, and by Jews in England and America before the version issued by the Jewish Publication Society of America in 1917. However, all traces of these assumed draft Septuagint translations have disappeared leaving only the Septuagint in itself. The Original Septuagint manuscript, too, has not been preserved. It may have perished during one of the anti-Jewish pogroms which occurred in Egypt under Roman domination, or when the great Library in Alexandria burnt down. Fortunately copies of the Septuagint had been made. In our own times, pending a census of what was destroyed in Europe during World War II, there are in existence some twelve manuscripts containing the Septuagint of the entire Old Testament and many hundreds containing individual divisions (the Pentateuch) or groups of books (The Minor Prophets, the Major Prophets) or individual books or fragments of part of single books. . . . The best known manuscript of the Septuagint is Codex Vaticanus (Vatican Library) dating from about C.E.[AD] 350. It is an extremely fine quarto volume of the finest vellum, written in an extraordinarily beautiful hand, and containing now 759 leaves (of which 617 belong to the Old Testament) out of an original total of about 820 leaves. Another of the famous manuscripts of the

Septuagint is Codex Sinaiticus . . . the [British] Museum is the owner of another fine and noted specimen of the Septuagint, of the 5th century, Codex Alexandrinus. Since the end of World War I, there have been discovered and published a group of Septuagint Manuscripts known as the Chester Beatty Papyri, dating in part from the second century A D. Numbers of fragments of individual books have also been brought to light in recent years, some of them (the Rylands Fragments of parts of some chapters in Deuteronomy) dating as early as about 150 B.C.E.[BC].[1]

Thus we know that even from this second source—the Septuagint—we have no full texts of the Bible earlier than the fourth century A D. In the light of that fact, it is easy to appreciate the great importance of two Isaiah texts discovered among the Qumran Scrolls. These texts are about a thousand years older than the oldest Hebrew text known to us and about five hundred years older than the earliest Greek version of the Septuagint. The lapse of time between our era and that of ben Asher and his disciples, is about the same as that between ben Asher and the date (a thousand years earlier) when the Qumran scrolls were copied. And the Isaiah scrolls found in Qumran were being copied only about six hundred years after the words were uttered by the prophet himself.

The great importance of the antiquity of the Dead Sea Scrolls, therefore, lies in the fact that they belong to the period in which no standardization of the holy scriptures had been effected. This is at once obvious by comparing the text of the scrolls with that of the translations on the one hand and the Masora on the other. What is astonishing is that despite their antiquity and the fact that the scrolls belong to this pre-standardization period, they are on the whole almost identical with the Masoretic text known to us. This establishes a basic principle for all future research on texts of the Bible. Not even the hundreds of slight variations established in the texts, affecting mainly spelling and occasional word-substitution, can alter that fact. On the other hand, as we learn from other

[1] *The Septuagint, the Oldest Translation of the Bible*, p. 8. (Cincinnati, 1949, Union of American Hebrew Congregations.)

manuscripts found in Qumran (for example that some pages from Samuel are particularly similar to that Hebrew text which must have served as a basis for the Septuagint translation but which was dissimilar to the Masoretic text) we discover that at that time, the first century BC and the beginning of the first century AD, there were several versions of Biblical books which differed from each other on major points. This now compels scholars to compare every part of the known Masoretic text with the corresponding places available in the Qumran scrolls. It should not, of course, be claimed that wherever there is a discrepancy between the two texts, the Isaiah Scroll should be given preference, since it is the older. But its minor variations, especially in details, are likely to guide the scholar when he reads the original text.

We now come to a description of the Isaiah Scrolls. There are two in Israel, one acquired by my father and one purchased from the Syrian Metropolitan in New York. The more complete of the two is the one acquired from the Metropolitan. We shall call it Isaiah MS 1. The scroll consists of fifty-four pages, or columns, containing the full sixty-six chapters of Isaiah, that is, both Books of Isaiah, as they are sometimes called. The scroll itself is made of seventeen leather sheets, sewn to each other with linen thread. The length of the sheets is unequal. The longest is 62·8 cm and the shortest 25·2 cm. The number of columns on each sheet also varies. Some have four columns, some three, and two sheets have only two columns. The complete length of the scroll is 7·34 metres. Its width is somewhat uneven, varying from 27 cm at its widest point to 24·5 at its narrowest. The number of lines on each column is also not constant. Some have 32 lines, some 31, some 30, 29, and 28. As with the other scrolls, its pages are ruled horizontally, and the writing hangs below the lines. These lines were most probably made, to quote Millar Burrows, with some 'semi-sharp instrument which tended to make a slight crease in the material frequently discernible on the back of the scroll'.

The scribe of this particular scroll was not one of the best. He made many mistakes, most of which, though, he himself discovered and corrected. Burrows points out, for instance, that in seven pages he found some forty-nine mistakes which the scribe corrected himself. However, several passages that were omitted by this scribe were later inserted by another, as is indicated by the different handwriting. In the margin running along the entire scroll are strange signs which seem to have been inserted later, and which are still unexplained. It is possible that they indicated passages or paragraphs that were of special significance to the members of the sect. Or perhaps they referred to the copying system of the scribe. There are many indications that this very manuscript was in use by the sect for quite a long time, and that parts of it which had suffered particularly from wear and tear had been already repaired in those days. Burrows describes it as follows:

Two bad tears of the parchment occurred in ancient times and were carefully repaired. One tear from the bottom of column twelve to within an inch of the top was sewed together with considerable skill, leaving little difficulty in reading the text. A tear from the top of the scroll diagonally part of the way across column eighteen, was repaired by covering the back of that part of the scroll with a thin piece of dark leather. . . . The first four and half columns had a thin strip of somewhat darker leather . . . placed along the top back edge to keep it from breaking away.[1]

The scribe used to separate paragraphs or secondary passages by leaving a space of one complete line or the blank end of an incomplete line. Of considerable interest is the fact that the chapter division in this scroll corresponds almost completely to the divisions in the text as we know it today, but there are in addition secondary divisions in the chapters themselves, which are marked in the same fashion. Most of the variations from the Masoretic text, as we have already

[1] *The Dead Sea Scrolls of St. Mark's Monastery*, Vol. I, p. xiv. (The American Schools of Oriental Research, New Haven, 1950.)

mentioned, are matters of spelling. But there are also minor textual variations, such as the interchanging of words and occasional minor differences in the actual text. The following are typical examples of such differences.

Chapter i. 15 of the Masoretic text reads: 'And when ye spread forth your hands, I will hide mine eyes from you. Yea, when ye make many prayers I will not hear: Your hands are full of blood.' Our scroll adds: 'and your fingers with crime.'

In chapter ii. 3, instead of: 'And let us go up to the mountain of the Lord, to the house of the God of Jacob,' the scroll has: 'And let us go up to the house of the God of Jacob.'

Another example is chapter ii. 9. Instead of: 'And the mean man boweth down, and the great man humbleth himself, therefore forgive them not', the text of the scroll drops the last four words. It also drops the whole of verse 10 in chapter ii: 'Enter into the rock and hide thee in the dust for fear of the Lord, and for the glory of His Majesty.'

To verse 2 of chapter iv: 'In that day shall the branch of the Lord be beautiful and glorious and the fruit of the earth shall be excellent and comely for them that are escaped of Israel,' it adds the words: 'and Judah'. In verse 5 it drops the words: 'And smoke by day and the shining of a flaming fire by night: for upon all the glory shall be a defence.' In verse 6 of the same chapter it drops the words: 'And there shall be a tabernacle for a shadow in the daytime.'

In chapter vi. 3 it says: 'Holy Holy is the Lord of Hosts' instead of the Masoretic: 'Holy, Holy, Holy, is the Lord of Hosts'.

In chapter xxi. 16 instead of: 'For thus hath the Lord said unto me, Within a year according to the years of an hireling, and all the glory of Kedar shall fail', the scroll has: 'Within three years. . . .'

And again in chapter xl. 12, where the Masoretic text says: 'Who hath measured the waters in the hollow of His hand and meted out heaven with the span, and comprehended the dust of the earth in a measure, and weighed the mountains in scales, and the hills in the balance?' the scroll says at the beginning: 'Who has measured the waters of the sea. . . .' In Hebrew this is a very minor alteration in the script (Waters of the sea = מי ים; waters = מים) but it seems a better rendition than the one understood in the Masoretic text, because of the more beautiful parallelism. Some other alterations have no parallelisms but several can be traced in the Septuagint.

The second scroll of Isaiah in Israel, one of the three acquired by Professor Sukenik, is known as MS 2. In contrast to MS 1, it is in a rather poor state of preservation. Here are Sukenik's own words on the subject:

The scroll was exceedingly difficult to unroll, for the columns were almost inextricably stuck together. . . . We found the surface of the scroll heavily smeared with a dark thick matter, presumably produced by the decomposition of the leather. In consequence many parts of the columns had grown so dark that only with great difficulty was it possible to make out traces of writing. Fortunately the scroll was legible in infra-red photographs. . . . This second Isaiah scroll has suffered particularly from the ravages of time. Only the upper part of the last third and a few fragments from the middle of the book have been preserved. The first of these fragments is from chapter x but only in chapter xxxviii do a number of fragments fit together to form several lines of writing. From this point on larger fragments appear which form a continuous strip of mutilated columns, and the quantity of preserved writing increases. The only sheet in this scroll that has not disintegrated is the penultimate, which consists of four columns, each one with an average of thirty-four lines. About fourteen lines are missing on the bottom of this sheet, which contained the words of the prophet from chapter lii to chapter lxi inclusive. Of the last sheet, which contained two columns, a fairly considerable amount of writing remains, but the sheet itself has disintegrated into numerous small fragments, and the writing is rather worn and difficult to read.[1]

In other words, if we count both the full pages and the

[1] *The Dead Sea Scrolls of the Hebrew University*, p. 30. Jerusalem, 1955.

mutilated ones, we find that MS 2 of Isaiah contains fragments of chapters

x	xiii	xvi	xix	xxii	xxiii	xxvi
xxviii	xxix	xxx	xxxv	xxxvii	xxxviii	xxxix
xl	xli	xliii	xlv	xlvi	xlvii	xlviii
xlix	l	li	lii	liii	liv	lv
lvi	lvii	lviii	lix	lx	lxi	lxii
lxiii	lxiv	lxv	xlvi			

Moreover in the excavations that were later conducted in cave 1 of Qumran, in which that scroll was originally discovered by the Bedouin, more fragments of the same MS 2 of Isaiah were revealed. These fragments are part of the first chapters, and are missing in Sukenik's MS.

Despite the incompleteness of this manuscript, its existence in parallel to MS 1 enables us to note significant comparisons. There are some differences. MS 2 is nearer to the Masoretic text known to us, especially in matters of spelling. It does not have the 'full' vowelled spelling that is common in MS 1. In addition it contains variations on the Masoretic text, not all of which appear also in MS 1. This is a further warning that we must be careful in our examination of and conclusion about the 'correctness' of these ancient scrolls, since they date back to the period before the final standardization which gave us the text as we know it today.

The variations between both texts and the traditional text, although many refer mainly to matters of spelling, in some places show versions similar to the Septuagint. The very existence of two different texts read by the same sect indicates the heavy responsibility and labour of those who later edited what is known as the Masoretic text. It may also be assumed that the sect possessed many manuscripts of the Holy Scriptures, which differed from each other in minor or major ways. However, although one should be cautious about all deviations from the Masoretic text, there is no doubt that in many cases these may be very useful in restoring the original text.

There is no question that the overwhelming significance of the texts lies in the fact that these scrolls, which are about a thousand years older than any Hebrew text hitherto discovered, vary only slightly from the text as it is known to us and used today. It thus proves the antiquity and authenticity of the Masoretic text.

Mention has already been made of the thousands of scroll fragments found in subsequent excavations in the caves, which according to the excavators represent most of the books of the Bible. It is not possible, within the limited scope of this book, to describe their contents and their differences from the Masoretic version. We shall be concerned here mainly with the seven complete Dead Sea Scrolls. We turn now to the next scroll, the Habakkuk Commentary, a unique work which, along with the commentaries on Psalms and Nahum, is a kind of transitional document between the scrolls which contain Biblical books and the non-Biblical scrolls.

CHAPTER 11

The Habakkuk Commentary

THE HABAKKUK COMMENTARY, one of the four scrolls purchased from the Syrian Metropolitan for the State of Israel, was at the time of its discovery the only work of its kind. Since then later excavations have revealed other similar commentaries on different Biblical books, although they have survived only in fragments. The Habakkuk Commentary is significant mainly in that it deals with the interpretation of the words of the prophet and attempts to apply them to contemporary events. The word repeatedly used by the writer of the Commentary is *pesher*, which is difficult to translate into English. It means a combination of interpretation, application and commentary. The writer, in other words, seeks to convey an understanding and interpretation of some concealed meaning in the prophecies, the true significance and application of which are known only to a chosen few. The Commentary of Habakkuk sets out to explain how the prophecies will materialize and how they should be applied to certain events of the day. Incidentally, this word *pesher* is one used often in the Aramaic part of the book of Daniel. An example of its typical use in connexion with the solution of the dream dreamt by Nebuchadnezzar (Daniel iv. 9) may help in an understanding of its meaning: 'O Belteshazzar, master of the magicians, because I know that the spirit of the holy gods is in thee, and no secret troubleth thee, tell me the visions of my dream that I have seen, and the interpretation [*pesher*] thereof.'

The author of the Habakkuk Commentary makes matters simple. His system is to quote verse by verse from the Biblical book of Habakkuk and immediately after it add his explanation, saying: 'Its hidden interpretation is such and such.'

The significance of the scroll is therefore two-fold. On the one hand it gives us the text of the book of Habakkuk, which, as mentioned before, is a thousand years older than any Hebrew text so far known. On the other, it enables us to learn of the background and problems of the members of the sect who wrote the scroll.

Before we proceed to a discussion of its contents, here is what Professor Burrows wrote on the state of its preservation when he first saw it:

The scroll was made of two strips of soft leather sewed end to end with linen thread. The hair side, on which the writing was done, was carefully dressed and is smooth to the touch; the obverse side was left undressed and is felt-like in texture. The thickness of the leather averages slightly more than half a millimetre. The smoothed surface was carefully ruled into lines and columns, with ruled margins between columns. The ruling was done with a sharp instrument, leaving a fine depression which is as evident to touch as to sight. Unfortunately the scroll is mutilated. An irregular line of disintegration or destruction extends through the entire length along the bottom. Hence at the bottom of each column a few lines of text are completely missing, while undulations along the edge of the break penetrate to varying depths into the text of the other lines. One portion at the beginning of the scroll has become dissevered from the rest. It contains portions of two columns, the left side of the first extant column and the right side of the second.[1]

The reader probably remembers how the Metropolitan sent the missing portion to us by mail, when it was discovered on signing the deed of purchase that it was missing.

Since the bottom part of the scroll is destroyed, it is very difficult to guess its original height. But according to Brownlee's meticulous calculations, it did not exceed 18 cm. It is also impossible to estimate the exact number of lines in each page. Again by calculation, it seems to have had an average of seventeen lines per page. The maximum height of

[1] p. xx. *The Dead Sea Scrolls of St. Mark's Monastery*.

one page, page 6, for instance, is 13·7 cm. The present length of the scroll is 141·9 cm. Since its end is preserved and only some of its beginning is missing, it seems that its original length must have been about 160 cm. The scribe of the Habakkuk Commentary seems to have been more experienced than the Isaiah scribe. His lines are straighter, his letters are very clear, and he made proportionately fewer mistakes. He leaves a small space between passages. This scroll is also devoid of marginal marks of the kind seen in Isaiah MS 1, except for some eleven X-like signs at the end of some lines. Another habit, characteristic of this scribe, is that when he had to write the Tetragrammaton (YHWH, the name of God), he uses ancient Hebrew script and not the one prevalent in the other scrolls. We do sometimes find in the other scrolls, though, that even the word אל (God) is written that way.

In spite of the missing parts at the beginning of the scroll, it is safe to assume that the 'interpretation' started with the first chapter and concluded with chapter ii. This is particularly interesting, since chapter iii differs from the other chapters by containing a prayer and many scholars, even prior to the discovery of the Dead Sea Scrolls, have been of the opinion that it is not an integral part of the original book.

The interpretation throws important light on two main subjects: the historical situation of Judaea in those times, and the problems that troubled the members of the sect on the shores of the Dead Sea. The first of these two subjects deals with the Kittim, who are expected to come from across the seas and threaten all countries of the universe. The second refers to the 'Wicked Priest' who was persecuting the 'Master of Justice' (or the 'Teacher of Righteousness'), the leader of the sect. Since the author of the interpretation proceeds in accordance with the verses of the book, he deals alternately and irregularly with both problems. But for the convenience of readers, we shall separate the subjects, and start with the Kittim.

To Habakkuk's words, *'For, lo, I raise up the Chaldeans, that bitter and hasty nation,'* the author of the scroll adds: 'Its hidden interpretation refers to the Kittim, who are swift and valiant in battle to destroy mighty rulers.'[1] The verse in Habakkuk *'which shall march through the breadth of the land'* he interprets: 'and they march over firm ground to smite and to despoil the cities of the land.'

To possess dwelling places that are not his. He is terrible and dreadful. His judgement and his might emanate from him. Its hidden interpretation refers to the Kittim, the fear and terror of whom are on all the nations, and in counsel all their purposes are to do evil and with deceit and guile they treat all the peoples. *Swifter than leopards are his horses—fiercer than the evening wolves, his horsemen sweep and spread from afar, they fly as the eagle that hasteth to devour ... they come all of them for violence; the set of their faces eastward.* Its hidden interpretation refers to the Kittim who trample the land with their horses and with their beasts, and from afar they come from the isles of the sea, to devour all the peoples, like an eagle without being sated. And it is with fury and with anger in wrath and vexation they speak with all the peoples, for that is what he has said: *With the set of their faces eastward, and they heap up as sand their captives ... and at kings he scoffeth and princes are a scorn unto him.* Its hidden interpretation refers to the fact that they are scornful towards the mighty and full with contempt towards the esteemed. Kings and princes they will ridicule and a mighty host they will scorn. *He derideth every stronghold and he heapeth up earth and taketh it.* Its hidden interpretation refers to the rulers of the Kittim who despise the fortresses of the peoples and laugh insolently at them and with a mighty host they surround them to take them and through terror and dread they are delivered unto their hands and they destroy them because of the iniquity of their inhabitants. *Then the wind passeth and disappeareth and he has made his might his god.* Its hidden interpretation refers to the rulers of the Kittim who according to the counsel of their house of guilt shall succeed each other; one after another they will

---

[1] In the following paragraphs the quotations from Habakkuk (which differ a little from the Masoretic text) are in italics and the interpretations of the author of the scroll in ordinary type.

come to destroy the peoples. *And he has made his might his god. . . .*

After talking about the end of the Gentiles, the author returns to the Kittim and in the commentary on chapter i. 16 we find one of the most helpful clues to their identification:

Therefore he sacrifices unto his net and burns incense to his seine [is interpreted]: That they sacrifice to their standards and their weapóns are the object of their worship.[1] *For by them his portion is fat and his food is plenteous.* Its hidden interpretation being that they spread their yoke and their tribute, their food, upon all the people year by year destroying many lands. *Therefore he empties his sword incessantly killing nations and has no pity.*[2] Its hidden interpretation refers to the Kittim who cause mighty to perish by the sword, young men and old, women and children and [even] on the fruit of the womb they have no mercy.

The author of the Habakkuk scroll thus takes all references to the Chaldeans and applies them to the Kittim of his times. We shall return to the problem of the Kittim when we deal later on with the scroll of the War between the Sons of Light and the Sons of Darkness and the Commentary of Nahum.

When the author writes about the problems that were troubling the members of his sect, he is most enlightening on the subject of the relations between the sect and the people of Jerusalem. Two central figures are mentioned, the Teacher of Righteousness and the Wicked Priest. About the first we read the following: '*That he may run that readeth it*. Its hidden interpretation concerns the Teacher of Righteousness to whom God has revealed all the mysteries of the words of His servants the prophets.' It seems, therefore, that the main quality of the Teacher of Righteousness is that he could interpret the words of the Prophets so that 'he may run that readeth it'. As for the Wicked Priest we read in the commentary on chapter ii. 5-6:

---

[1] Most probably referring to the Romans.

[2] The commentary has 'Harbo' sword instead of 'Hermo' net, in the Masoretic text.

Yea indeed wealth will lead the haughty man to betray and he will not stop who enlarged his desire as Sheol and he is insatiable as death. For gathered unto him are all the nations and all the peoples are assembled before him! Yea all of them will utter a proverb against him and interpreters of riddles he shall have and they shall say woe to him who increases what is not his! How long will he impose upon himself a pledge. Its hidden interpretation concerns the Wicked Priest who was called by the name of truth when he first took office, but when he ruled over Israel his heart was lifted up and he abandoned God and betrayed the statutes for the sake of wealth; and he stole and assembled the wealth of men of violence who had revolted against God; and he took the wealth of peoples thus adding upon himself the guilt of transgression; and ways of abominations he wrought in all impurity of uncleanness.

Both figures had naturally their own assistants and followers. The writer applies verse 3 of chapter ii to the followers of the Teacher of Righteousness of whom he says:

If it tarry wait for it because it will surely come; it will not delay. Its hidden interpretation refers to the men of truth, the doers of the Law [Torah] whose hands do not slack from the service of the truth [even] when the final appointed time is delayed for them. For all the appointed times of God will arrive in their due time in accordance with what He has decreed for them through the mysteries of His prudence.

Farther on he says of them:

Its hidden interpretation concerns all the doers of the Law in the house of Judah, whom God will deliver from the House of Judgement for the sake of their toil and their faith in the Teacher of Righteousness.

On the other hand he refers also to the assistants of the Wicked Priest as for example in chapter ii. 8:

Because thou hast spoiled many nations, all the remnant of the peoples shall spoil thee. Its hidden interpretation refers to the last Priests of Jerusalem, who gathered wealth and loot from the spoil of the peoples but at the end of the days their wealth with their spoil will be given unto the hands of the army of the Kittim.

Thus we learn of the punishment that will befall the Wicked Priest and the last priests of Jerusalem when the Kittim arrive. The author of the scroll is angry at the Wicked Priest not only for his sinful deeds generally, but also, perhaps mainly, for his persecution of the Teacher of Righteousness. Chapter ii. 15, which is very obscure in the Masoretic text, he renders thus:

Woe to him who maketh his neighbours drink the eruption of his anger, yea even intoxicating drinks so as to look upon their festivals. Its hidden interpretation refers to the Wicked Priest who has persecuted the Teacher of Righteousness in order to destroy him through the anger of his wrath, in the house of his exile; and at the time of the feast, on the resting of the Day of Atonement, he appeared unto them in order to destroy them and to cause them to stumble on the day of the fast, their Sabbath of rest.

It seems from the above that the Wicked Priest physically persecuted the Teacher of Righteousness who was in exile. Moreover he did so on the Day of Atonement. It is difficult to believe, however, that any priest, even the most wicked, would choose the Day of Atonement for acts of persecution. This strengthens the theory which is based on other premises that the calendar used by the sect was not identical with the calendar prevailing in Jerusalem. The Day of Atonement near the Dead Sea would not, therefore, coincide with the official Day of Atonement. It may even be that this was one of the causes of the persecution.

The tyranny of the Wicked Priest was not conducted against the Teacher of Righteousness alone. It was directed against the sect as a whole. This may be assumed from what the commentator says about verse 17 of chapter ii:

Because of men's blood and for the violence of the land, of the city, and of all that dwell therein: Its hidden interpretation refers to the Wicked Priest, so that he may receive his retribution for what he has exacted from the poor . . . him shall God condemn to destruction, as he plotted to destroy the poor . . . The city is Jerusalem, wherein the Wicked Priest wrought works of abomination and defiled the Temple of God.

It seems that during those persecutions some individuals betrayed the Teacher of Righteousness by failing to help him when they could. Chapter i. 13 reads:

Why do ye look oh traitors and why dost thou remain silent when the wicked devoureth one who is more righteous than he! Its hidden interpretation refers to the House of Absalom and the men of their party, who kept silent when the Teacher of Righteousness was reproached and did not aid him against the Man of Falsehood, who had rejected the Law in the midst of their whole congregation.

The bitter end of the Wicked Priest symbolized to the sect the realization of the other prophecies of Habakkuk. In a second interpretation of ii. 8 we find:

His smiting with the penalties of wickedness and horrible and terrible diseases they executed upon him and acts of vengeance upon the corpse of his flesh; or: Its hidden interpretation refers to the Wicked Priest, whom because of the wrong done to the Teacher of Righteousness, and the men of his party, God delivered him unto the hands of his enemies to torment him with smiting that he might be destroyed in bitterness of soul, for the evil he had done to His elect ones.

Similarly in another instance, he mentions the Preacher of Falsehood (ii. 12-13):

Woe to him that buildeth a town with blood and establisheth a city by iniquity! Behold, is it not of the Lord of Hosts that the peoples shall labour for fire and nations weary themselves for vanity? Its hidden interpretation refers to the Preacher of Falsehood, who misled many into building a city of vanity through bloodshed and into forming a congregation through lies for the sake of his glory, to compel many to toil in labour of vanity and to make them pregnant with works of lies, and thus their labour will be to no avail, and they will enter the judgements of fire, because they have cursed and insulted the elect ones of God.

This most interesting and significant scroll, therefore, reveals the internal and external political situation of the time of its writing. On the one hand the Kittim threaten to conquer all nations and to conquer Jerusalem, which the writer considers a punishment which its priests fully deserve. On the other hand we witness a cruel struggle between the Teacher of Righteousness—the sect's leader—and his followers, against the Wicked Priest—the sect's enemy and persecutor—who dwells in Jerusalem and finally gets punished for his misdeeds. Who was the Teacher of Righteousness? Who was the Wicked Priest? Who were the Kittim? These three questions are the main problems which research on the scrolls seeks to solve. They have not yet received a definite answer, though various solutions have been suggested. These will be discussed in the last chapter of this book.

The fragments of the Commentaries which were discovered after the Habakkuk Scroll came to light deal mainly with the minor prophets and the Psalms. It is unfortunate that they were found incomplete. But the little we have of them is of importance both for an understanding of the internal problems of the sect that wrote them and the date of the writing, as well as for the additional light they shed on Biblical texts. The more important of them are the Psalms and Nahum Commentaries.

CHAPTER 12

The Commentary on Psalms and the Commentary on Nahum

OF THE two remaining commentaries of which enough fragments were discovered to enable a reconstruction of their contents, let us first mention the Commentary on the Psalms. This was discovered in Cave 4, and those parts of it published up to date, are written on two pieces of skin measuring ten by twenty centimetres and five by nine centimetres respectively. A third fragment of the same Commentary was only very recently published. The fragments contain a Commentary on Psalm 37, similar in style to the Commentary on Habakkuk and in all probability written about the same time. Its subject is of course influenced by the nature of Psalm 37, which deals with the victory of the just over the wicked and the meek over the evil-doers. This subject, as will be seen later, is very close to the beliefs of the sect and its way of life, and could easily be applied to the persecution of the Teacher of Righteousness, the sect's founder, by the Wicked Priest, who wished to kill him.

Since we have already discussed at length the Commentary on Habakkuk, it seems sufficient here to quote the three fragments fully, and let the reader see for himself the obvious resemblances. The importance of the Psalms Commentary lies in its biographical data about the Teacher of Righteousness, which confirms that he was a priest, as the Habakkuk Commentary implied: 'its hidden interpretation refers to the Priest, the Teacher of Righteousness, who . . .' and 'its hidden interpretation refers to the wicked ones of Ephraim and Manasseh who will seek to attack the Priest and the men of his counsel'. It is also interesting to note several sentences, which will be discussed later when dealing with the scroll of the War of the Sons of Light against the Sons of Darkness, such as: '. . . the penitents of the wilderness who will live a thousand generations' describing members of the sect living in the Judaean desert, or: 'Its hidden interpretation refers to all the wickedness at the end of the forty years when they will be no more, and there will not be found in the earth any wicked man' expressing their belief, also described in the 'War' Scroll, that at the end of the days all Sons of Darkness would be annihilated in a battle which would last for forty years. Also significant are the terms used to denote the sect: 'Those who Return to the Law', 'The Community of His Elected Ones', 'The Community of the Poor'. The Psalms Commentary refers to the leaders of Jerusalem in similar terms to those used in the Commentary on Habakkuk: 'the Princes of wickedness who have cheated His holy people.' And in the light of what the Commentary on Habakkuk says about the Wicked Priest in reference to the Day of Atonement, there is special significance in the following sentence: 'Its hidden interpretation refers to the Congregation of the Poor who adhere to the Appointed Day of Fast and they will be delivered from all the snares. . . .'

As with the Commentary on Habakkuk, here too, we may learn their version of Psalm 37. The reader who compares the Masoretic text with that of the Psalms Commentary will find several interesting differences both in writing and text. But let the scroll speak for itself:

Passage 1
. . . Will perish by the sword, and by hunger, and by plague. *Cease from anger and forsake wrath and be not inflamed with a fury to do evil, for the wicked will be cut off.* Its hidden interpretation refers to all those who return to the Law, who do not refuse to repent of their wickedness, for all those who refuse to repent of their iniquity will be cut off. *And those who are waiting for the Lord will inherit the earth.* Its hidden interpretation: they are the Con-

gregation of His Elect Ones who do His will. *And in a little while the wicked will be no more and I shall look carefully for his place and it will be gone.* Its hidden interpretation refers to all the wickedness at the end of the forty years when they will be no more, and there will not be found in the earth any wicked man. *And the humble shall inherit the earth and they shall delight in the abundance of peace.* Its hidden interpretation refers to the Congregation of the Poor who adhere to the Appointed Day of Fast and they will be delivered from all the snares . . .

Passage 2
1. *The wicked have drawn out the sword and have bent their bow; to cast down the poor and the needy,*
2. *And to slay the upright of way. Their sword shall enter into their own heart and their bows shall be broken.*
3. Its hidden interpretation refers to the wicked ones of Ephraim and Manasseh who will seek to attack [literally: to put forth a hand]
4. the Priest and the men of his counsel in the time of trial which is coming upon them. And God will redeem them
5. from their hand and afterwards they shall be given into the hand of terrible ones of the Gentiles for judgement.

Passage 3
. . . The penitents [literally: those who return from] of the wilderness who will live a thousand generations . . . men and to their seed for ever. *And in the days of famine they will be satisfied but the wicked will perish.* Its hidden interpretation is that He will keep them alive in famine in the appointed period . . . will perish in famine and in plague all who do not . . . *and those who love the Lord are like the preciousness found by miners* [?] Its hidden interpretation . . . the Congregation of His elect ones which will be chieftains and princes . . . sheep in the midst of their flocks. *All of them will be consumed like smoke.* Its hidden interpretation refers to the Princes of wickedness [?] who have cheated His holy people, who will perish like the smoke. . . . *The wicked man borrows and does not repay but the righteous person is gracious and giving. For those whom He blessed will inherit the earth, and those whom He had cursed will be cut off.* Its hidden interpretation refers to the Congregation of the Poor . . . the inheritance of all the . . .

they will inherit the Mount of the Height of Israel . . . and His holy people will delight . . . *will be cut off*, they are the ruthless . . . the wicked of Israel, who will be cut off and will be destroyed for ever. *By the Lord are man's steps secure and all his ways does he delight; for though he fall he will not be hurled headlong, for the Lord is supporting his hand.* Its hidden interpretation refers to the Priest, the Teacher of [Righteousness who] has established him to build for Him a Congregation of. . . . *A lad was I and now am I old and yet I have not seen a righteous man forsaken nor his seed seeking food. All the day he is gracious and lends and his seed is a blessing. . . .*

Passage 4

1. *The wicked watcheth for the righteous and seeketh to [slay him. The Lord will not leave him in his hand, nor] condemn him when he is judged!*
2. Its hidden interpretation refers to the Wicked [Priest] who [. . . . . .] to slay him [. . .] and the Law
3. which he sent to him. But God will not [leave him in his hand] nor [condemn him when] he is judged. And [God will] repay to [him] his recompense
4. into the hand of terrible ones of the Gentiles to do to him [. . .]

Among the remaining Commentaries, the most important is no doubt that of Nahum, which has recently been published; it alone (as yet) mentions historical characters with their true names, and offers a clue to the identification of the Kittim and the date of composition of the Commentaries.

Moreover, this Commentary—which mentions, among other things, the hanging up of people alive—has caused a storm in the Christian world, since several scholars have hinted that the description of the alleged hanging of the Teacher of Righteousness was reminiscent of the crucifixion of Jesus.

This fragment (published in June 1956 in the *Journal of Biblical Literature*, by Mr J. Allegro of Manchester University) was acquired in the spring of 1955 from members of the Ta'amira tribe, and is part of other fragments of the same

Commentary discovered in Cave 4. All those fragments together constitute some four to five pages of that Commentary. The passage published by Allegro, which is the most
important of all, contains the first page of the scroll found up
to now, and interprets what is said in Nahum chapter ii. This
Commentary too, like the others, differs in places from the
Masoretic text, and the reader can judge that easily for
himself:

1. A dwelling for the wicked ones of the Gentiles. *Whither the
   lion, the lioness, went, the lion's cub* (or: *Whither the lion went
   to bring the lion's cub*)
2. [*And none to terrify*]. Its hidden interpretation refers to
   [Deme]tris, King of Greece, who sought to enter Jerusalem
   by the counsel of the Seekers-after-Smooth-Things.
3. [. . .] The kings of Greece from Antiochus until the appearance of the rulers of the Kittim, and then will be trodden
   down.
4. [. . .] *The lion tears sufficient for his cubs and strangles for
   his lioness prey.*
5. [Its hidden interpretation] refers to the Lion of Wrath who
   smites with his mighty ones and the men of his counsel.
6. [. . . *and he filled with prey*] *his hole and his den with ravin.*
   Its hidden interpretation refers to the Lion of Wrath [who
   inflicts punishment of (?)] death on the Seekers-after-Smooth-
   Things, who hangs men up alive
8. [. . .] before in Israel, because the one hanged alive [. . .]
   is called (the accursed of God). *Behold I am against thee*
9. *saith the Lord of Hosts and I shall burn up in smoke thy
   multitude and the young lions the sword shall devour. And I
   shall cut* [*off from the land*] *his prey*
10. [. . .] and *thy multitude,* they are the battalions of his army
    [. . .] and his *young lions,* they are
11. [. . .] and his *prey,* it is the wealth which the [pries]ts of
    Jerusalem gathered together which
12. [. . . E] phraim, Israel will be given to [. . . . .]

Who was this Demetrius who wished to come to Jerusalem?
Who were the Seekers-after-Smooth-Things, who asked him

to come? Who was the Lion of Wrath who hanged people alive? Is this an indication of the hanging of the Teacher of Righteousness? These are the main questions aroused by this Commentary. And although the Commentary has raised new problems, it has also answered two of the main questions: the identification of the Kittim and the earliest date which it is possible to attribute to the writing of the Commentaries, namely the period of Demetrius, King of Greece.

We shall leave the discussion of these questions to the last chapter, which will deal with the identification of the sect and its period.

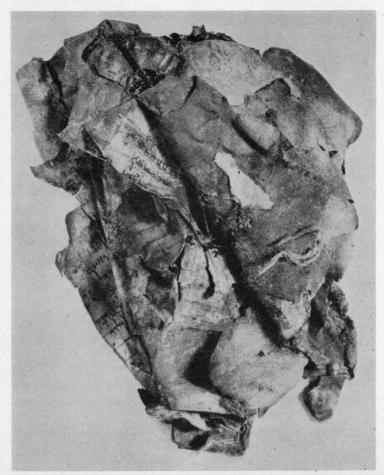

Part of the Thanksgiving Scroll before unrolling

CHAPTER 13

The Thanksgiving Hymns

THE SCROLL of the Thanksgiving Hymns stands between those scrolls which contain Biblical books or interpretations of Biblical books, and those which deal with the code of the sect. This scroll is one of the three purchased by my father, Professor Sukenik. It was originally found in two parts, and additional fragments complementary to it were later discovered in excavations of Qumran Cave 1. The first part consisted of three sheets, each containing four columns. These sheets, strangely enough, were found rolled separately and not one within the other as with the other scrolls. All bear similar marks of decay in the same position of the sheet, suggesting that for a length of time they were rolled in a continuous single scroll form and later re-rolled in the separate form in which they reached us. The second part contained some seventy fragments of leather, some small and some larger. All were stiff and thickly stuck together. The indications are that it was probably already in a poor state at the time the scroll was hidden, and that it was concealed in haste.

Altogether twelve almost complete columns have been preserved; six additional columns are partly defective, and with varying degrees of deterioration; and there are seventy separate fragments, some containing as many as twenty lines of script and others bearing little more than a few letters. Like the other scrolls, this one too has some columns which are easily readable with the naked eye, and others which can be deciphered only with the aid of infra-red photography, since parts are covered with some dark excretion resulting from the decay of the leather.

This scroll was obviously worked on by two scribes. The

first was clearly an expert. He has a beautiful handwriting and he seems to have taken great care in the forming and spacing of his letters. He wrote the word 'God' occasionally in the ancient Hebrew, also called the Phoenician script, and occasionally in the ordinary Hebrew script of the scrolls. The second scribe, on the other hand, has a crude and ugly handwriting and leaves not enough space between words. This scribe started his work on the twenty-second line of page eleven, and wrote his first few words above those of the first scribe.

Since none of the top margins and only some of the bottom margins of the pages have been preserved, it is difficult to determine the number of lines on each page. However, from the lines that are left it is evident that this was one of the tallest scrolls written, since some pages still contain more than forty lines. The measurements of the three complete sheets are 61 × 32 cm, 62 × 31 cm, and 56 × 31 cm. The fourth incomplete sheet is some 43 cm long. The original scroll was certainly three metres in length at the very least.

On the contents of the scroll, here is what Professor Sukenik, the first to handle it, wrote:

The Thanksgiving Scroll is a collection of songs, expressing the views and feelings of one of the members of the sect whose writings were discovered in the Dead Sea Genizah [manuscript repository]. Imitating the style of the Psalms, the songs express thanks for the acts of kindness God has performed for their author. Since the great majority begin with the phrase 'I thank thee, O God', I have called the entire group the Thanksgiving Scroll. About thirty-five whole and fragmentary chapters of Thanksgiving hymns have survived. Most of the hymns strike a distinctive personal note. Of particular interest from this viewpoint is the long chapter in column 4, in which the author refers to himself as a man who hoped for special revelations from God and who, despite his opponents, had many followers flocking to him to listen to his teaching. A possible inference is that the author was the Teacher of Righteousness often mentioned in these scrolls as well as in the Zadokite Document of the Damascus Covenanters. His complaint over being compelled to leave his country—'he thrust me out of my land like a bird from its nest' (Column 4 line 9)—corresponds to the statement in the Habakkuk Commentary that the Wicked Priest forced the Righteous Teacher into exile from the country. (Column 11 line 6.)'[1]

The apparent similarity between the Thanksgiving Scroll and the Book of Psalms, owing to their resemblance in style and expression, is only external. The nature of their contents makes the one completely different from the other. The Thanksgiving Scroll is an individual, religious literary creation, written by the leader, or one of the leaders, of the sect, in which he combines pronouncements on the principles of his belief with purely autobiographical details. Not knowing the original length of the scroll, it is quite possible that this writer composed numerous additional hymns, which were written on additional sheets and which have not yet been found. The reader will recall that in the letter of Timotheus I to the Metropolitan of Elam (about AD 800) he writes that he was told by Jews who had found scrolls in caves near the Dead Sea: 'We have found more than two hundred Psalms of David among our books.' The reference may well have been to these Thanksgiving Hymns.

At all events we should be grateful that age has dealt kindly with this scroll and has thus preserved for us not only a document of major historic and religious value, but also a precious literary creation.

Let us try and summarize the contents of the hymns and offer a few translations which may convey their character and import more effectively than a prosaic explanation.

The first chapter of the first column on the first complete sheet is a hymn of glory to the all-powerful Lord who is 'forbearing in judgement' and right in all His deeds, and who had knowledge of the acts of all mankind before He created them. Nothing has been, is or will be done without His premeditation. He created the creatures of the earth and the

[1] *The Dead Sea Scrolls of the Hebrew University*, p. 39.

heaven and the angels above, and determined their duties in His realm. He created the luminaries and the stars and their mysterious and wonderful ways. He ordained the laws of lightning, of thunder, and of rain. He created in His wisdom the earth, the seas, the depths and the rivers. He created man, and ordained all his deeds before he came into existence. The all-powerful God thus created all according to a preconceived plan. None of His deeds is changeable. And even those things which seem strange to humans have been created with a definite purpose.

In the second hymn, the writer explains that he understands all these mysteries because God has revealed them to him. He thanks God for this, since he himself is only flesh and blood and undeserving of such privilege. He says of himself: 'I am the product of clay and the fashioned of water; the filth of the genitals and source of menstruation; the melting pot of iniquity and the frame of sin (of) the twisted and perverse spirit without understanding.'

The writer knows that everything has been pre-ordained by God for all the days to come. Therefore humans must not complain of His deeds, even when they seem unjust, for God is the God of knowledge, justice and truth, while humans are only sinners. Even those humans who are pious in their ways are so only because God has strengthened them against all evil-wishers. God made the strong weak and to the weak He gave support, strengthening their loins and their lips. The writer then goes on to talk about himself, saying that God has strengthened his soul in the midst of evil and has thus turned him into a snare for sinners and a restoration for penitents. Because of his struggle for the ways of truth he has become an object of persecution to all evil-doers, who attack him like a gale upon high seas. Nevertheless he continues to serve as a guide to the pious and to expound to them the secrets of creation: 'Thou hast appointed me a banner for the righteous chosen and interpreter of knowledge in wondrous mysteries.' This phrase gives added support to Sukenik's theory that the writer of the hymns was the Teacher of Righteousness himself.

In the next hymn the writer thanks God who has strengthened him in his fight against his evil persecutors:

I thank Thee, O Lord,
For Thou hast placed my soul in the bundle of life
And Thou shelterest me from all the snares of the pit
And from the violent who seek my soul
Because I adhere to Thy Covenant;
But they are an assembly of naught
A congregation of Belial
They do not know that from Thee is my firm stand
And that through Thy mercies Thou wilt save my soul,
For by Thee my course is ordered
Thou hast caused them to gather against my soul
So that Thou mayst be glorified through the judgement of the
    wicked
And thus Thou hast fortified me against the sons of men
For Thy mercy is with me
And I said, mighty men have encamped against me
All around with all their instruments of war.
They have hurled fatal arrows
And the glittering of (their) lance (was)
Like fire which devours the wood
And like the roaring of many waters was the tumult of their voices
A splashing flood bringing destruction for many
. . .
But I, though my heart melted like water,
My soul was strengthened through Thy covenant.
Their feet entangled in the net which they have spread for me
And into the snares which they have hidden for my soul they
    have themselves fallen
And my foot stood on a firm and level ground.

In another hymn he says (column 3):

I thank Thee, O Lord,
For Thou hast delivered my soul from the pit
And from Sheol Abaddon Thou hast brought me up again to
    the top of the world.

And I walked on an endless firm plain
And I knew that there was an abode
For him whom Thou hast formed from the dust for eternal
    assembly,
Thou hast purified a perverse spirit from a great sin,
So it may take its position among the host of holy ones
    [angels]
And to come together with the congregation of the Sons of
    Heaven
Thou hast allotted to (each) man an everlasting lot [or portion]
Among the spirits of Knowledge,
To praise Thy name together in joyful song
And to relate Thy wonders in all Thy deeds [or works].

In another hymn he goes on to thank God who served him as a 'wall of strength' in all his troubles. One of the stanzas of this hymn is important in giving even clearer support to the thesis that the author may have been the Teacher of Righteousness himself. He writes:

For he has driven me from my country like a bird from its nest.
And all my friends and acquaintances were thrust afar from me
And they thought I was like a lost vessel.
And they, the interpreters of lies and prophets of guile,
They formed against me plots of Belial
Wanting me to barter Thy law which Thou hast engraved on my
    heart
For the flatteries which they address to Thy people.

What a forceful autobiographical description this is, showing the lot of the writer banished from his country and his struggle for truth against evil.

The next hymn describes again the writer's battle with his fierce enemies and how, with the help of God, he has succeeded in continuing to preach His teachings. This hymn also reveals that his opponents were sometimes even members of his own sect:

And I became . . . an object of quarrel and strife among my
    friends,

Jealousy and anger to those who entered into my covenant,
And all those who assembled around me grumbled and
　　complained . . .
Those who eat my bread lifted up their heel against me,
And all those who joined my party have cast aspersions upon me
And the men of my community turned rebellious and grumbling
　　round about.

The burdens of the writer are heavy, his troubles grave and insupportable. These troubles darken his days. But his faith in God is unwavering and he knows that his enemies will come to a bitter fate for at the end of the days God's mighty sword will annihilate all evil.

He continues in this vein throughout the hymns, telling alternately of his suffering and of the succour he derives from his faith in God, who has revealed to him the secret of truth in spite of the fact that he is only made of clay (p. x, 3-14):

But I am of dust and ashes,
What can I plan—unless Thou hast wished it
And what can I devise without Thy desire?
How shall I strengthen—unless Thou hast established me?
And how can I be wise unless Thou hast created me!
How could I talk—unless Thou hast opened my mouth?
And how may I answer—unless Thou hast made me wise?

The many biographical notes woven into the hymns, the great faith expressed in them about the writer's destiny and duty as the bearer of truth and the interpreter of God's words; the description of the distress and misfortunes that have befallen him; and the fact that the hymns are written in the first person—all these tend to strengthen the conviction that the author of these Thanksgiving Hymns, was, in fact, the Teacher of Righteousness. What was the way of life of the sect which he headed? And about what did he preach? Answers to these questions appear in still other writings of the sect, preserved in the scrolls.

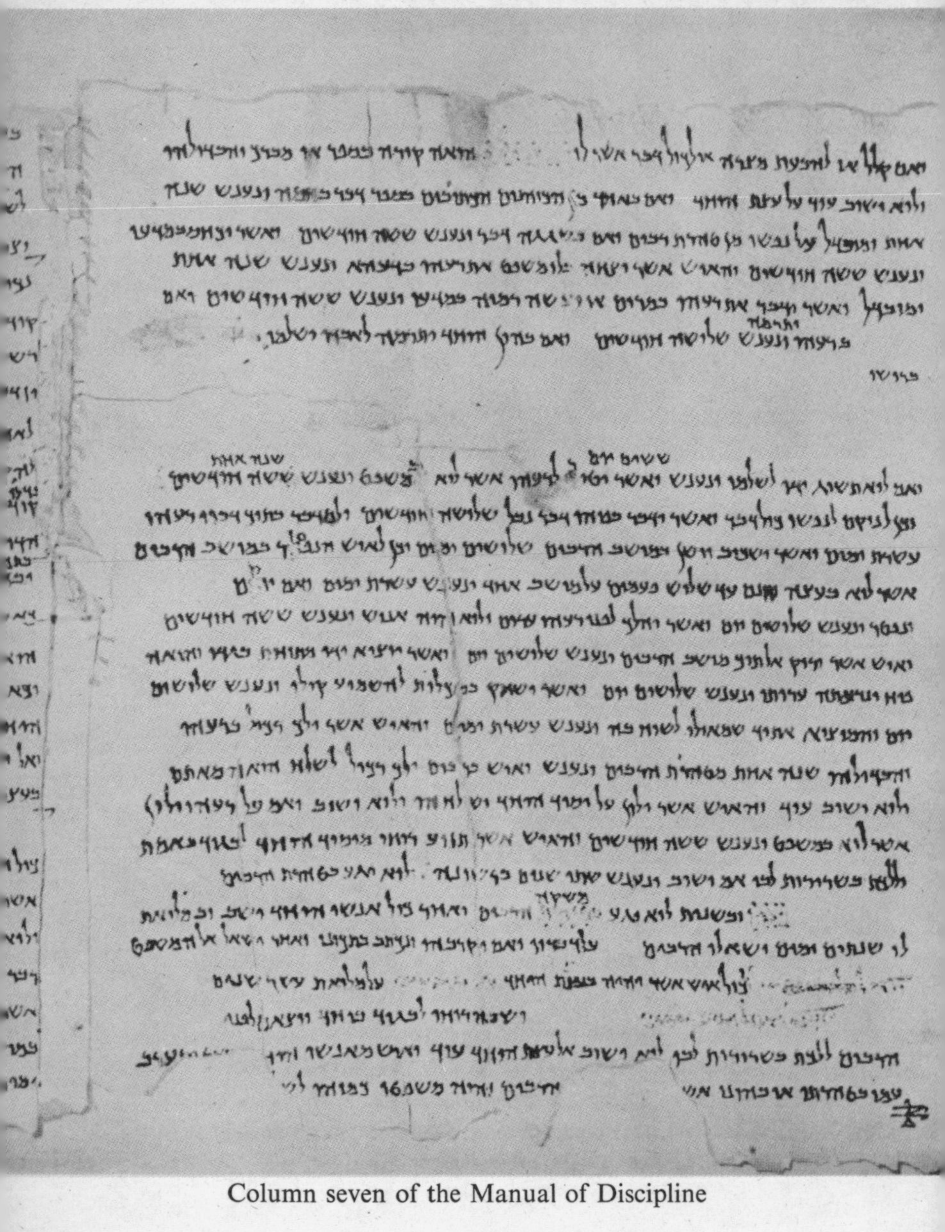

Column seven of the Manual of Discipline

PART IV

CHAPTER 14

The Manual of Discipline or the Rule of the Community, and the Damascus Covenant

HAD THE discoveries in the Dead Sea caves been confined to Biblical books alone, it is doubtful whether we should now have any information about the community whose scribes copied the holy works. We should know nothing of its special nature, or even that it was different from contemporary communities. We would not even have been able to assume that the books belonged to a particular sect and not just to ordinary inhabitants of the area in which they were discovered.

True, the Commentary on Habakkuk and the Thanksgiving Scroll tell us clearly that these writers, who were busy interpreting the holy scriptures in their own special way, were people who had serious complaints against the inhabitants of Jerusalem and their priests, and that their Teacher of Righteousness was persecuted and had been compelled to flee from the Wicked Priest. But from these books alone it would not be possible to establish with finality that these people constituted a special religious sect. Such assumptions based on the Commentary of Habakkuk or the Thanksgiving Hymns could only be indirect.

To our great good fortune, however, among the parchments discovered in the Dead Sea area was a scroll which contains nothing less than the detailed code of rules of the sect, expounds the principles of their faith, outlines their system of accepting new members, records the punishment of recalcitrant members, and provides a general description of the sect's way of life. This scroll is called the Manual of Discipline (or the Rule of the Yahad). It was found in Qumran Cave 1, together with the other six scrolls. This scroll, though very full, shows signs of being incomplete. It comprises eleven pages with an average of twenty-six lines to a page. It is about two metres long and its height is twenty-five centimetres. These eleven pages are written on five sheets. From the many late erasures, corrections and additions it is apparent that the scroll had been used by the sect over a long period. Incidentally, a few pages from a scroll that seems also to have been found in Qumran Cave 1 were recently published in England. All the signs point to these pages having formed part of the original complete Manual of Discipline.

The first page of the scroll in the possession of the State of Israel, which is evidently not the original beginning of the scroll, is devoted entirely to the initiation ceremonies of new members into the covenant of the community. At the same time it makes reference to the principles of their faith which, in brief, are rules of behaviour in accordance with the laws of God, given 'through Moses and through all His Servants the prophets'; that is: 'to love all that He has chosen and to hate all that He has rejected; to keep away from all evil and to adhere to all good deeds; to do truth and righteousness and justice in the land, and not to walk any longer according to the stubbornness of a guilty heart and eyes of fornication, doing all evil.'

All those who are accepted as members are 'Sons of Light', and they pledge themselves 'to love all Sons of Light, each according to his lot in the Council of God, and to hate all Sons of Darkness, each according to his guilt in the vengeance of God'.

The code proceeds to explain that the members are required to contribute to the community 'all their knowledge and strength and wealth into the Yahad [literally: the together or community] of God'.

They must thus contribute everything they have. The sequence of these contributions is interesting—knowledge, strength and wealth: that is, from the relatively permanent to the transitory.

But before the writer describes the ceremony itself he emphasizes another principle to which the members of the sect must adhere without fail: 'Not to advance their times or delay any of their appointed periods.' This is a clear injunction that they must keep rigidly to the special calendar of the community.

A description of the ceremony itself follows: as a first step, the novices must swear 'not to turn away from following Him because of any dread or trial which might occur in the dominion of Belial'. After that, 'when they enter into the Covenant, the Priests and the Levites shall bless the God of Salvation and all His deeds of truth, and all those who are entering into the Covenant shall say after them "Amen! Amen!" ' In the course of the ceremony the Priests bless the Lot of God while the Levites curse the Lot of Belial and particularly Belial himself. At the end of these utterances all members of the community respond with 'Amen! Amen!'

Here are translations of some typical portions of both blessings and curses which seem to me to illustrate the general style of the scroll and to convey an idea of the nature of the sect and of its beliefs. Here is the first blessing by the Priests:

May He bless thee with every good
And keep thee from all evil
And enlighten thy heart with the wisdom of life
And grant thee eternal knowledge
And turn His face of mercies towards thee for eternal peace.

This is followed by the Levites' curse:

Cursed be thou in all thy evil and guilty deeds.
May God make thee an object of horror
In the hand of all the avengers of vengeance
And may He condemn you for destruction
In the hand of all those who pay retributions.
Cursed be thou without compassion

As like darkness are thy deeds
And damned be thou in the gloom of eternal fire.
May God not pardon thee when thou callest on Him
And may He not forgive thee for thine iniquities.
May He lift up His angry face for vengeance upon thee
And mayst thou have no peace
At the mouth of all those who adhere (to the law) of the Fathers.

This initiation ceremony seems to have been an annual event, conducted in the days of the dominion of Belial. During the ceremony the members dressed themselves in accordance with some established order, thus:

This shall they do every year, all the days of the Dominion of Belial: The Priests shall be first to march past in formation, one after another according to their spiritual seniority. And the Levites shall march after them and all the people shall march thirdly in formation one after another by thousands, and hundreds and fifties and tens.

This scroll does not specify in detail how the ceremony is arranged or how the people are organized in their thousands and hundreds. But from the scroll known as The War of the Sons of Light against the Sons of Darkness, which forms the subject of the next chapter, we know that they used standards and trumpets which must also have been in use in these acceptance ceremonies.

In the third page of the Manual of Discipline we find a condemnation in rather strong terms of all those who refuse to become members of the Covenant of God. Let each of them know that:

He will not be purified with the water for impurity and he will not sanctify himself with seas and rivers, and he will not be made clean with any water for washing. Unclean, unclean will he be as long as he despises the commandments of God.

This is the only right way:

by the spirit of uprightness and humility all his sins will be atoned, and by the submission of his soul to all the ordinances of

God, his flesh will be purified for the sprinkling with water for impurity . . . and he will establish his steps to walk perfectly in all the ways of God . . .

Pages 3 and 4 of the scroll go on to define in detail the problems of Light and Darkness. This seems to be the standard original definition, for even the other scrolls, including the War of the Sons of Light against the Sons of Darkness, when referring to these problems, base themselves mainly on the description in the Manual of Discipline or some earlier as yet unknown source.

From the God of knowledge is all that is and that is to be; And he established all their designs before they came into being, And when they come into being, in a manner preconceived, according To His glorious design, their work will be accomplished not to be changed; in His hand are the ordinances of all, and He provides for them all their needs. And He created man to have dominion over this world, and He made for him two spirits by which to walk until the period of His visitation. They are the spirits of Truth and Perversion; In the abode of Light are the offsprings of Truth, and from the source of Darkness the offsprings of Perversion.

In the hand of the Prince of Light is the dominion over all Sons of Righteousness—in the ways of Light they walk; And in the hand of the Angel of Darkness is all dominion over the Sons of Perversion—in the ways of Darkness they walk.

But through His mysterious will, God causes the Angel of Darkness to mislead all men of righteousness and make them sin 'till His appointed time'. On the other hand:

The God of Israel and His Angel of Truth have helped all the Sons of Light . . . for He created the spirits of Light and Darkness and upon those spirits he founded every deed and upon their ways every service, and upon their ways every service [note the repetition of the same phrase twice, which is of course not a scribal error, as some scholars maintain, but refers to the two ways, the way of Light and the way of Darkness]. . . . The one of them God loves eternally and He is pleased with all its accomplishments; As for the other He abhors its company and all its ways He hates for ever.

In the process of describing the ways of Light and Darkness the scroll goes on to say:

But God in the mysteries of His knowledge and His glorious wisdom has fixed a period for the existence of Perversion; and at the fixed time of Visitation He will destroy it for ever. Then truth will come forth forever on earth.

Later we learn that in the opinion of members of the sect, the time of the victory of Truth over Perversion and Light over Darkness is not very distant. Indeed, the scroll of the War of the Sons of Light against the Sons of Darkness is devoted to the preparations for and a description of that battle.

From page 5 onward the Manual of Discipline deals mainly with the code governing the life of the members of the community. It starts off with the words: 'And this is the disposition for the men of the Yahad who volunteer to turn from all evil and to hold firmly to all that He has commanded according to His will, and to separate themselves from the congregation of perverse men, and to be united in matters of the Law and property.' The members of the sect are examined and categorized according to their wisdom and record of action; in the words of the scroll: 'according to his knowledge and his deeds.' Their names are thus registered in order of a certain priority, so that it should be known who is senior and who is junior, that 'the lesser obey the greater'. This order of priority is not permanent 'and their spirits will be re-investigated as well as their deeds each year, so as to elevate each one according to his knowledge and the perfection of his way, or to put him back according to his perversions'. Their life is completely communal: 'Together they shall eat and together they shall pray; together they shall counsel.' Then comes a description of the procedure of how 'together they shall eat': 'and when they set the table to eat or the wine to drink, it will be the Priest who will stretch out firstly his hand to bless the first portion of the bread or the wine'. This description, incidentally, is surprisingly similar to the customs of the Essenes as described by Josephus.

Following the rules governing the communal meals the scroll enumerates the rules of conducting meetings: 'A man shall not speak in the midst of his neighbour's words, before his brother finishes speaking . . .' —and 'the man who is asked shall speak in his turn'. At certain sessions a man must be careful of his words: 'A man shall not speak a word which is not to the liking of the superiors' and 'any man who has a word to say to the superiors, the man shall stand up on his feet and say: I have a word to say to the superiors; if they tell him, he shall speak'.

Most interesting is the prescription for judgement and punishment of members of the sect. For example:

If there is found among them a man who lies about his wealth intentionally, they shall exclude him from the midst of the purified (place) of the superiors (or the public) for one year and he shall be deprived [literally: punished] of a fourth of his food [literally: bread]. . . . And he who answers his fellow in stubbornness, or speaks with a quick temper, . . . he shall be punished for one year . . . and if he has spoken in anger against one of the priests registered in the book . . . he shall be punished a year and set apart for himself. . . . But if he spoke unintentionally, he shall be punished six months . . . and if he shows himself negligent so as to cause damage to the property of the Yahad, he shall repay it in full; but if he is not able to pay it he shall be punished sixty days. . . . One who bears a grudge against his fellow without justification, shall be punished six months [inserted above the words 'six months' in the scroll, are the words 'a year'] . . . And he who shall utter an obscene word shall be punished three months. And for him who breaks into the words of his fellow—ten days . . . and he who shall lie down and sleep in the public session—thirty days. . . . And he who shall walk naked before his fellow without being gravely ill [or: without having to do so] shall be punished six months; A man who will spit in the middle of the public session will be punished thirty days. . . . And he who shall laugh foolishly and loudly shall be punished thirty days. . . .

And so the code of rules goes on to list punishments for libel against a private individual, libel against the public and so on. The judgements mark a clear difference between intentional crimes and those committed in error. It is also clearly emphasized that these are the rules by which members should conduct themselves during the Dominion of Belial and 'until there shall come a prophet and the anointed ones of Israel and Aaron'. The leaders of the sect however did not concern themselves with writing rules only for the Days of Belial. They also prepared regulations for the 'end of the days'. Thus we find on the one hand an entire scroll dealing with the future war—to take place on the day decided upon in advance by God—between the Sons of Light and the Sons of Darkness, and on the other we find a code for the behaviour of all the people of Israel in the end of the days, since it was believed that that period was not far off and members should already be informed of the regulations then to prevail. The 'end of the days' code was written on two pages of this same Manual of Discipline but these two pages were found separately (though in the same cave) and later published by the Oxford University Press. It starts off with the words:

And this is the disposition of the whole community of Israel at the end of the days. . . . And when they shall come they shall assemble all those who shall arrive, even children and women, and they shall read to them all the laws of the Covenant in order that they shall understand all their laws lest they shall err.

It then goes on to list the duties of a citizen of Israel according to his age. He should be taught the Books of the Law and its ordinances from childhood, or rather from the moment he is capable of grasping their meaning: 'according to his days they shall enlighten him.'

This enlightening period might last some ten years. When he reaches the age of twenty, he passes from the group of children to that of the 'mustereds'. Until that age, a boy is not permitted to marry. At the age of 25 he receives his first appointments in the duties of the community and in holy work. At the age of 30 he is mobilized into the army. This division of the ages is very similar to the one described in the War Scroll. There too, men are not mobilized before the age of 25 and even then only for the services. Only at the age of 30 do they become fighting soldiers. The War Scroll, though, adds many more details, such as the specific ages for the cavalry, light infantry, and heavy infantry.

Just as the Manual of Discipline begins with a description of the procedure at communal meals in the days of Belial conducted by the Priest, so, in these two pages setting out the 'end of the days' code, we find a description of the communal meal, in which, naturally, the two heads of Israel—the Priest and the Prince—participate. Moreover, in another fragment, also apparently belonging to this same scroll, we find two blessings, one for the anointed priest and one for the anointed Prince of the Community, and a third blessing for 'the sons of Zadok, the priests'.

This Manual of Discipline, then, provides definite information on all matters concerning ceremonies, punishments and rules of the sect, or of that part of the sect, at least, which lived communally on the shores of the Dead Sea. There is fortunately in existence an additional book, known as the Damascus Covenant, which also deals with the ceremonies and rules of the sect. It may be found fruitful to add a word about this interesting and important document, even though it was not one of the scrolls found in the Dead Sea discoveries.

The Damascus Covenant was actually first discovered in 1896 in the famous Genizah of the ancient Synagogue in Cairo, by the well-known Jewish scholar, Solomon Schechter, who at the time was a lecturer on the Talmud at the University of Cambridge. This Synagogue was founded in the year 882. In 1896 a Genizah (a storechamber in a synagogue for disused sacred books and documents) was brought to light there. It contained thousands of documents and manuscripts, prominent among them the Hebrew manuscript of Ecclesiasticus. The vastness of the find of Talmudic, Biblical and other books eclipsed to some extent the significance of the Damascus Covenant (named by Schechter on its discovery 'Fragments of a Zadokite Work'). But when it was published in 1910 the peculiar contents of the document provoked an acute debate among scholars, reminiscent of the debates over the Dead Sea Scrolls. Indeed most of the opinions expressed by scholars today about the identity of the Dead Sea sect and its date follow closely what was written and said after the discovery of the Damascus Covenant.

Professor Sukenik was the first to point out that the style and contents of the Damascus Covenant were very similar to the style and contents of some of the Dead Sea Scrolls. He therefore suggested that the Covenant be considered as one of the books belonging to the Dead Sea sect. This suggestion was not only accepted by most scholars, but was unexpectedly confirmed through the discovery in the Qumran caves of some fragments (as yet unpublished) belonging to other copies of the same book.

The manuscript discovered in the Cairo Genizah was of course a late copy, approximately of the tenth century AD. It was not even written on a scroll, but in book-form (codex). The question arises of how the book came to be found in the Cairo Genizah. The same question may also, perhaps, be applied to some of the other documents found in the Synagogue, notably the manuscript of Ecclesiasticus. There may be some validity in the view that the book reached the community during the discovery of scrolls on the shores of the Dead Sea at the beginning of the ninth century, of which we have learned through the letter of Timotheus I, Patriarch of Seleucia. The Cairo Genizah yielded two manuscripts of the Damascus Covenant: the first consists of sixteen pages and its end is missing; the second has two pages only. The Covenant is divided into two principal parts; one recounts the history of the sect, the other, like the Manual of Discipline, contains a large number of rules and customs.

The first part begins by describing the destruction of the First Temple which is said to be due to the crimes of Israel, which has deserted God. But God, remembering 'the Covenant of the forefathers, caused a remnant to remain of Israel and gave them not up to be consumed'. Then, 390 years after the conquest of Nebuchadnezzar, God remembered them 'and caused to grow forth from Israel and Aaron a root of cultivation to possess His land and to wax fat in the goodness of His soil'. For twenty years after that they 'were like the blind and like them that grope their way' until 'He raised up for them a Teacher of Righteousness to lead them in the way of His heart'. But in the last generation Israel rebelled and then 'the man of scoffing who preached to Israel waters of falsehood, caused them to go astray on a trackless chaos'. As a result they sinned, and 'justified the wicked and condemned the righteous' and 'incited [anger] for quarrel among the people' until God 'laid waste all their multitude'.

The writer then proceeds to tell 'all those who enter the Covenant' the principles of the sect's belief, which is similar to that expounded in the Manual of Discipline. On the third page he gives a short history of Israel since the days of Noah and his sons, and all that happened to them in the times of Abraham, in Egypt, in the desert and after.

From there he continues in the method of the Commentator quoting a sentence in the Bible and following it with a commentary. For example the sentence from Ezekiel (xliv. 15): 'But the priests, and the Levites, the sons of Zadok, who kept the charge of My sanctuary when the children of Israel went astray from Me, they shall come near to Me to minister unto Me, and they shall stand before Me to offer unto Me fat and blood,' is followed immediately by his own interpretation: 'The Priests are they that turned (from impiety) of Israel, who went forth from the land of Judah; and (the Levites) they that joined themselves with them and the

Sons of Zadok are the elect ones of Israel . . . who shall arise and serve in the end of the days.'

This and similar paragraphs were the reason why Schechter, when first seeing this book, called it 'Fragments of a Zadokite Work'. But this is of course misleading. The constant repetition that the priests must be descendants of the Sons of Zadok, is only one of the proofs that the sect was in opposition to the Priests of Hasmonean (Maccabean) descent.

The writer then goes on to denounce the sins of Israel and Judah 'during all these years' when 'Belial will be let loose upon Israel', when 'whoredom', 'wealth' and the 'pollution of the sanctuary' were prevalent, and men permitted themselves to take two wives 'whereas the foundation of the creation is a male and a female He created them' and those who went into the Ark 'two and two they went into the Ark'.

Moreover he severely condemns the people of Israel who defile the Temple and pay no heed to the words of the Torah 'but lie with her who sees the blood of her flux and they marry each his brother's or his sister's daughter. . . . And with the tongue of blasphemies they opened the mouth against the ordinances of the Covenant of God saying: they are not established'.

Yet when the country was destroyed, the sins of Israel reached their nadir, and the leaders misled the people and thus brought on the destruction of the land. But God, remembering again the Covenant of the Ancients:

He raised from Aaron men of understanding, and from Israel men of wisdom and He caused them to understand. [And they dug] a well which princes dug, which the nobles of the people delved with the staff; [the interpretation of this is that] the well is the Law (or the Torah) and those who dug it are they that turned (from impiety) of Israel who went out from the Land of Judah and sojourned in the Land of Damascus . . . and the Legislator (the staff) is the searcher of the Law . . . and the nobles of the people are those who come to dig the well with the staffs which the legislator (the staff) prescribed, to walk in them during the whole period of wickedness, and without them they shall not grasp (instruction) until the arising of him who will *teach right-eousness* at the end of the days.

Thus we learn that when the people left the Land of Judah for the Land of Damascus, their (new) leader demanded that they follow the rules of the Covenant until the end of the days, when the Teacher of Righteousness will arise anew.

In the same way the author interprets the saying from the Book of Numbers in the song of Bile'am: 'A star shall step forth out of Jacob, and a sceptre shall rise out of Israel' to mean 'The star is the searcher of the Law who came to Damascus . . . the sceptre is the Prince of the whole congregation'.

The above quotations show clearly why scholars named the book the Damascus Document or the Covenant of Damascus.

Parts of the Damascus Covenant contain regulations governing all spheres of life in the various camps in which the sectarians lived, reminiscent in many respects of those enumerated in the Manual of Discipline. These parts start with the words: 'And this is the disposition for the judges of the Congregation;' the judges will be ten in number, chosen from the congregation—four from the Tribe of Levi and Aaron and six from Israel—and they will have to be 'instructed in the book of the *Hagu* [possibly the Torah] and in the foundations of the Covenant'. The ages of the judges are specified too: from 25 to 60 years old. The author offers an interesting explanation as to the 60 years' age limit: 'And let no one over sixty any longer set himself up to judge the congregation; for when man transgressed, his days were diminished and in the heat of God's anger against the inhabitants of the earth He commanded that their knowledge should depart from them before they complete their days'.

As will be seen in the next chapter, the War Scroll also fixes the maximum age for service in any military capacity at 60. Later comes the 'disposition for those that settle in camps;

those that walk in these ways during the period of wickedness, until there shall arise and serve the anointed one(s) of Aaron and Israel.'

From parallels in the Manual of Discipline we know this to mean the *two anointed* ones, the religious head and the lay head. Settlers in these camps should not be less than ten in number, and will be organized by thousands, hundreds, fifties and tens, just as is specified in the Manual of Discipline and the War Scroll; that is, they are organized in militia fashion. Wherever there are ten men there shall also be a priest 'instructed in the book of *Hagu*' and 'according to his words shall they all be ruled'.

The regulations also provide for cases where the priest is not 'well instructed' in the book. When this occurs, 'all the members of the camp shall be ruled according to the decision of a man of the Levites well instructed in all these'. In addition every camp will have a man to act as controller or overseer, as is evident from the words 'and this is the disposition for the controller of the camp'. The controller's duty is to supervise the daily life and behaviour of members. There is also a chief controller to supervise all controllers, called 'a controller who is over all the camps' who is 'from thirty to fifty years old'.

The rules lay down that all members must be registered by name according to some order; 'The priests first, the Levites second, the (lay) Israelites third and the proselytes fourth.'

The last page in our possession from this book contains important information on the relative date of its authorship. It says: 'The exact list of their fixed periods—of which Israel is blind—behold is specified explicitly in the Book of the Divisions of the periods according to their Jubilees and their Weeks.' There is hardly any doubt that the writer refers to the famous Book of Jubilees. This is one of the pseudepigraphical books, which like many other books of that group greatly influenced the sect's way of thought, and today it may even be assumed that it was compiled by the precursors of the sect.

From these two documents, the Manual of Discipline and the Damascus Covenant, we learn that the members of the sect, whether living co-operatively on the shores of the Dead Sea or whether dispersed in settlements all over the country, led an organized and special way of life in accordance with their own individual rules, recorded in books written for that very purpose. The sect was not only composed of priests and Levites but also of ordinary lay Israelites. In all religious matters they were ruled by the priest or, when there was none, by the Levites; their lay affairs were supervised by a controller. They had thus created a substitute for the rules and regulations commonly observed by the Jews governed from Jerusalem at that time, and had come closer, in their opinion, to the way of life of the tribes of Israel in the period of their wandering through the wilderness. Meanwhile they awaited the moment when all evil, sin, and darkness would disappear from the world, and justice and light would prevail. The advent of that time was not far off, in their view, and required preparatory organization and planning.

This planning and organization are described in another wonderful and unique scroll, known as the War of the Sons of Light against the Sons of Darkness.

CHAPTER 15

The Scroll of the War of the Sons of Light against the Sons of Darkness

THE WAR SCROLL is one of the seven scrolls found in Qumran Cave 1, and one of the three scrolls purchased by the late Professor Sukenik from the antiquities dealer in Bethlehem for the Hebrew University. This scroll is a hitherto unknown book, and there is none like it, either Jewish or Christian, in the literature of the time of the Second Temple or in the period following. Nor is there any work like it among the sect's own books.

A word first about the physical state of this scroll. When it reached us after its discovery, it had nineteen pages, written on five sheets. There were four pages on the first sheet, six on the second, five on the third and three on the fourth. Of the fifth sheet one page only was left and it was difficult to determine its original place on the sheet. But among some small fragments discovered later in the cave, after the removal of the first scrolls, there is one at least which fits nicely into page nineteen. On it one can decipher a few letters of the following page. This proves that the scroll originally had at least twenty pages. The end of the scroll is missing but its beginning is intact; that is clear from the empty page adjoining the first written column on its right which clearly served to envelop the scroll when rolled.

This scroll, like others, is worn at the bottom, due to the dampness which penetrated the clay jar in which it was found. The damaged edge is wavelike in shape and so one page has more lines than another. We calculate that each page originally had an average of twenty lines.

The scribe excels in the beauty of his handwriting. Like some of the other scribes, he ruled his pages with the aid of some sharp-edged instrument: horizontally for the lines, and vertically between columns, where he also left a margin. The letters themselves are written below the lines and not above as is usual today. Between paragraphs he left the space of a line or more.

Although he seems to have been a master craftsman, mistakes can nevertheless be detected in both spelling and text. Most of these errors were corrected by the same scribe or by later readers. The overall length of the scroll in its present state of preservation is approximately 2·90 metres.

As we have observed when describing the Manual of Discipline, the Scrolls sect believed in the division of all human creatures into Sons of Light and Sons of Darkness. Members of the sect itself, naturally, belonged to the Sons of Light; their enemies belonged to the Sons of Darkness. The sect, as we have shown, concerned itself not only with rules of behaviour during the days of Belial, but gave thought also to the problems of the coming victory over the Sons of Darkness at the end of the days. When would that victory occur, how would it happen and what preparations were necessary for it? The author of the scroll believed that that day was near, simply because he knew that victory would come at 'a time of mighty trouble for the people to be redeemed by God. In all their troubles there was none like it'. He bases his assumption on the passage in Daniel xii. 1: 'And at that time shall Michael stand up, the great prince which standeth for the children of Thy people; and there shall be a time of trouble, such as never was since there was a nation even to that same time. And at that time thy people shall be delivered.' Considering the troubles that have befallen the members of his sect to be the 'trouble such as never was', it is clear to him that salvation is imminent.

Although he knows that delivery and victory will be caused by God through His angel Michael, with the Sons of Light actively participating in the fight against the Sons of Darkness and their protecting angels, he believes that regulations for that future war need to be laid down now and the Sons of Light must be taught the ways of war, both those specified in the Bible and those prevalent at his time, so that they may use them to advantage. His central point is that the war will take place only on the day appointed in advance by God, and only the Sons of Light who keep all the rules specified in the Bible as understood by them shall participate on the right side. If they will be pure in this sense, then God will make them victorious in the end. The author therefore considers it necessary: (a) to define who are Sons of Light and who are Sons of Darkness; (b) to establish when the war will take place; and (c) to lay down the general plan for that war and decide the details of tactics, weapons, and army organization on the one hand, and to enumerate the Biblical rules for the conduct of war and their application to this war on the other.

The importance of the scroll springs both from its contents and its purpose. For the first time we find comprehensive data on military regulations in the Jewish armies during the late period of the Second Temple, containing military technical terms hitherto unknown. The scroll also brings to light a number of very beautiful prayers to be recited at various stages in the war, most of which were also unknown up to now. And since the sect sought to follow the pattern of organization of the tribes of Israel during their sojourn in the wilderness, as described in the Book of Numbers, we have here a magnificent opportunity of studying that organization and of comprehending some of the unclear passages in the Biblical account. It is true, of course, that the author of the scroll and his sect lived a long time after those Biblical events; but they were still some two thousand years closer to them in time than we are. The description of the tactics and the names of the enemies are also of help in fixing the date the scroll was written, since the author no doubt based his descriptions of tactics and weapons on what he saw around him, or perhaps read about, in his own time.

We come now to the contents of the scroll, following the order set by the author. He begins with the first stage of the future war which will be against 'the Sons of Darkness, the army of Belial, the troops of Edom and Moab and the Sons of Ammon and the army of the dwellers of Philistia and the troops of the Kittim of Asshur, and in league with them the Offenders against the Covenant'.

The Edomites, Ammonites, Moabites, and Philistines are the peoples immediately surrounding the land of Israel, and were its traditional enemies. But the Kittim are undefined. The name must of course have been known to members of the sect at the time, although it has a different connotation at different periods. The Kittim have already been mentioned in the Commentary on Habakkuk, but they will be discussed in greater detail in the chapter dealing with the sect and its period. It should also perhaps be explained that by the 'offenders against the Covenant' the author means the enemies of the Sons of Light from within the Jewish people. This is the only reference to them in the whole scroll. The other listed enemies are all Sons of Darkness, whom the Sons of Light will fight in the first round.

The Sons of Light are defined as 'the Sons of Levi, the Sons of Judah and the Sons of Benjamin, the exiles of the wilderness'. The definition 'exiles of the wilderness' seems very appropriate for those Sons of Light who lived most of the time in the desert of Judah. The first round of the war will take place 'when the exiles of the Sons of Light return from the wilderness of the peoples to encamp in the wilderness of Jerusalem'. The term 'the wilderness of the peoples' is taken from Ezekiel and seems to refer—in contrast to the 'wilderness of Jerusalem'—to all the other members of the sect living in countries of the diaspora, and especially Syria. The next stage of the war will be against the Kittim of Egypt and the one after that will be against 'all the kings of the north'.

The victory will bring 'deliverance for the people of God and eternal annihilation for all the Lot of Belial'. But the author immediately warns that the final battle in which both men and angels will participate, will not be easy 'and three Lots shall the Sons of Light prove strong to smite the wicked and in three the army of Belial shall recover to reverse the Lot of the Sons of Light . . . but in the seventh Lot shall the great hand of God subdue Belial'.

The congregation as a whole will fight against the Kittim and their allies, but the war against the Kings of the North will be conducted by divisions serving in turn. The plan is simple enough and quite comprehensible. The first group of enemies is the most dangerous to the Sons of Light, since they are geographically nearest their territory and within the boundaries promised to Abraham; the Kings of the North are farther away. The war will last forty years altogether—similar to the forty years' sojourn of the tribes of Israel in the wilderness. There will be no fighting on Sabbatical years, so that there will be only thirty-five fighting years. The war of the congregation as a whole, against the Kittim and their allies, will take six years of fighting; the war against the Kings of the North, twenty-nine years. The war plans give exact details of the names of the various enemies and how long the Sons of Light will have to fight each of them individually:

In the first year they shall fight against Aram Naharayim; in the second against the Sons of Lud; in the third they shall fight against the remainder of the Sons of Aram, Uz, Hul, Togar, and Masha, which are beyond the Euphrates; in the fourth and fifth they shall fight against the sons of Arpachshad; in the sixth and seventh they shall fight against the Sons of Ishmael and Keturah. In the ten years after those, the war shall spread out against all the Sons of Ham according to their families in their dwelling places. In the remaining ten years the war shall spread out against all the Sons of Japhet in their dwelling places.

After describing the general war plan and the division of the years accorded to each enemy, the author proceeds to explain the rules of battle, the dispositions as he calls them. He begins, naturally enough, with the rules enumerated in the Bible, such as those of the trumpets and standards, basing his writings mainly on the most important Biblical source for those matters, the Book of Numbers, x:

And the Lord spake unto Moses, saying: Make thee two trumpets of silver; of a whole piece shalt thou make them; that thou mayest use them for the calling of the assembly, and for the journeying of the camps. And when they shall blow with them, all the assembly shall assemble themselves to thee at the door of the tabernacle of the congregation. And if they blow but with one trumpet, then the princes, which are heads of the thousands of Israel, shall gather themselves unto thee. When ye blow an alarm, then the camps that lie on the east parts shall go forward. When ye blow an alarm the second time, then the camps that lie on the south side shall take their journey: they shall blow an alarm for their journeys. But when the congregation is to be gathered together, ye shall blow, but ye shall not sound an alarm. And the Sons of Aaron, the Priests, shall blow with the trumpets; and they shall be to you for an ordinance for ever throughout your generations. And if ye go to war in your land against the enemy that oppresseth you, then ye shall blow an alarm with the trumpets; and ye shall be remembered before the Lord your God, and ye shall be saved from your enemies. Also in the day of your gladness, and in your solemn days, and in the beginnings of your months, ye shall blow with the trumpets over your burnt offerings, and over the sacrifices of your peace offerings; that they may be to you for a memorial before your God: I am the Lord your God.

These rules served as a starting point for the description of the use of trumpets in the war of the Sons of Light. Here too, the priests blow the trumpets, and different trumpets and signals are used for different actions. But the system of signals is far more elaborate and technical. The trumpets described in the War Scroll are divided into two groups: ceremonial trumpets and fighting trumpets. All bear special inscriptions and slogans in keeping with their purpose. In the first group of trumpets are those 'for the calling of the congregations' bearing the inscription 'The God-summoned'; trumpets 'for the calling of the Commanders' with the inscription 'Princes of God'. There are 'trumpets of the levies' with the inscription 'Band of God'; 'trumpets of the camps' with the inscription 'peace of God in the encampments of His saints'; and 'trumpets of the expedition of the camps' with the inscription 'God's mighty deeds to scathe the enemy and to put to flight all opponents of justice and disgraceful retribution to the opponents of God'.

The war trumpets, however, are classified according to the tactical stages of the fighting and the order of battle. Thus the 'trumpets of the battle arrays', bearing the inscription 'Arrays of God's battalions for His wrathful vengeance upon all Sons of Darkness', serve as a signal to start off the battle arrays. The writer even describes the sound of this trumpet blast—it is 'level' or 'even'. For the assembly of the 'men who fight between the lines', that is, the skirmishers, there were special 'trumpets for calling the skirmishers' with the inscription 'Vengeful remembrance for the appointed time of God'. The sign to commence the fighting proper was given with 'trumpets of killing' and their inscription was 'The hand of God's might in battle to strike down all sinful slain', and their sound was 'high-pitched and intermittent'. Then there were 'trumpets of the ambush' inscribed 'Mysteries of God for the perdition of the wicked'. The signal for pursuit of the enemy is given with special 'trumpets of pursuit' inscribed: 'God has smitten all Sons of Darkness. His wrath shall not cease until they are annihilated'. Similarly there are trumpets for withdrawing the fighting forces, entitled 'trumpets of withdrawal' with the inscription 'God hath gathered', the sound of which is 'low, level, and legato'.

All these trumpets are blown by six priests, specially attired, who move about the units at the front. In addition there are many horns used by the Levites and other members of the congregation for the purpose of frightening the enemy. These war cries are given only at the beginning of the battle.

The author of the scroll devotes much space to the description of the banners carried by the congregation both when setting out to war and during the stages of the actual fighting. This description, too, is based mainly on the passage from Numbers ii. 2: 'Every man of the children of Israel shall pitch in his formation [marked] by banners according to their father's house; far off about the Tabernacle of the congregation shall they pitch.' According to the scroll, every unit has its own banner: 'The great banner at the head of all the people' was fourteen cubits long. It is inscribed, 'people of God, Israel and Aaron', as well as the names of the twelve tribes of Israel according to their order of birth. Similarly the heads of the camps of the 'three tribes' have their own banner, and so have the myriad, the thousand, the hundred, the fifty and the ten. There are altogether eight kinds of banners, the longest of which reaches fourteen cubits and the shortest seven. Each banner carries the name of the commander of the unit, and the smallest of all—the unit of ten—carries 'the name of the commander of the ten and the names of the nine men appointed to his charge'. Thus the names of all members of the congregation were recorded. This served also during ceremonies, when the people were organized according to some established order. In addition to these basic inscriptions, denoting the nature of the unit, there were three categories of slogans, attached to the banners, appropriate to the various stages and progress of the fighting: 'When they go to battle'; 'when they close in for battle', and 'when they withdraw from battle'. Thus the great banner had the slogan 'Congregation of God' when going to battle; 'Battle of God' when closing-in for battle; and 'deliverance of God' when returning from battle. In the same way the banners of the heads of the camps had the slogans 'Camps of God', 'Vengeance of God' and 'Victory of God', respectively for the three stages, and the banners of the tribes had 'Tribes of God', 'Cause of God' and 'Help of God'. The banners of the myriads had 'Families of God', 'Retaliation of God',

'Support of God', and the banners of the thousands had 'Battalions of God', 'Strength of God' and 'Joy of God'. The banners of the hundreds carried the slogans 'Assembly of God', 'Retaliations of God' and 'Thanksgiving to God', and the banners of the fifties had 'Those summoned by God', 'Might of God' and 'Praise of God'. Lastly, the banner of the ten in its three stages, had the slogans 'Hosts of God', 'Annihilation by God upon all Sons of Vanity' and 'Peace of God'.

These were the inscriptions and slogans of the congregation in general. But the tribe of Levi and its families (the priests), sons of Kohath, Gershon and Merari, had their own banners, on each of which they wrote the name of the chief of the family (Prince of Kohath, etc.) and the names of the commanders of his thousands. The Levites, too, changed their slogans according to the stages of war. When they went to war the sons of Aaron wrote 'Truth of God'; when they closed in they wrote 'Right hand of God' and when they returned they wrote 'Exalt God'. The sons of Kohath carried the following slogans during the three stages: 'Justice of God', 'Appointed day of God' and 'Magnify God'. The Sons of Gershon had 'Glory of God', 'Panic of God' and 'Praise of God', and the banner of Merari had 'Judgement of God', 'Slain of God', 'Glory of God'.

The sub-units of the priests' families, such as the units of thousand, hundred, fifty and ten, had their own inscriptions: 'Anger of God in wrath against Belial and all men of his Lot without remnant' followed by the name of the commander of the thousand and the commanders of his hundreds; 'Hundred of God for battle against all unjust flesh', followed by the name of the commander of the hundred and the commanders of his fifties: 'Ceased is the conclave of the wicked by the might of God' followed by the name of the commander of the fifty and the commanders of his tens; and lastly 'Rejoicing of God upon the ten-stringed lyre' followed by the names of the commander of the ten and his men.

As with his descriptions of the trumpets and banners, the author spares neither effort nor word in describing the organization of the army and its weapons. The infantry has two groups: heavy infantry or 'formations of the front' and light infantry to be used as skirmishing battalions and called the 'battalions in between'. The 'formations of the front' are seven in number, each composed of three thousand men sub-divided into three one-thousand units. There is thus a total force of twenty-one thousand. Each formation when forming up parades in seven arrays. Their ages are between 40 and 50 years and they are uniformly armed with shields (made of copper burnished like a face-mirror), 2·5 cubits long, 1·5 cubits wide, that is some hundred and fifteen by seventy centimetres. Each also has a spear, three hundred and sixty centimetres long, and a sword about seventy centimetres in length. The shields, spears, and swords are all decorated. The light infantry, however, or the 'battalions in between' are seven thousand in all, divided into seven units, and their ages are between 30 and 45. Since they skirmish before the main battle starts, they are not uniformly armed. Each group has different weapons, to suit the different ranges, as follows: two units of slingers; one unit of lancers and shield bearers; one unit of swordsmen and shield-bearers; three units of javelin throwers, each soldier armed with seven javelins. In other words the overall weapon strength of the heavy infantry was twenty-one thousand spears and twenty-one thousand swords; the strength of the light infantry was two thousand slings, twenty-one thousand javelins, a thousand lances and a thousand swords.

The scroll is full of details concerning the method of fighting during the various stages of battle. First, all units array themselves in formations for the purpose of roll-call and prayer. Next, the fighting units deploy in two lines, four formations in front and three at the rear. Between the formations there are intervals to allow the passage of the light infantry, who at the beginning array themselves behind the 'formations of the front'. When a special signal is blown, the skirmishing phase begins with two units of slingers. Next, also to the sound of a special signal, comes the turn of three units of javelin throwers, who after throwing seven javelins return to their posts. Then, when the fighting closes up, two units of shield and lance bearers set out and, their duty done, return to their places. At certain stages of the battle, and if one of the units is defeated, a reserve unit is immediately sent out as replacement.

In addition to the twenty-eight thousand infantry, heavy and light, the army of the Sons of Light has six thousand cavalry. These, too, are grouped into light and heavy cavalry. The light cavalry has four thousand six hundred riders, fourteen hundred of whom fight together with the light infantry—two hundred riders to every thousand of infantry, one hundred on either flank. The rest of the light cavalry are stationed at the rear and on the flanks. The heavy cavalrymen number fourteen hundred. They are called the 'cavalry of the men arrayed in the front formations' and they fight alongside the heavy infantry. The six thousand cavalrymen are recruited from the twelve tribes, five hundred from each. The age of light cavalrymen is the same as for the light infantry, between 30 and 45, and the heavy riders are between 40 and 50. Most interesting is a description of the quality of the horses, which should be 'male horses fleet of foot, tender of mouth, long of wind, full in the measure of their years, trained for battle and accustomed to hearing noises and to all sights and spectacles'.

The author then goes on to describe the regulations for changing the order of battle and disposition of the formations in accordance with the the tactical needs of different situations. He starts by saying, 'This is the disposition of changing the arrays of the battle units' which have the following names: 'Long rectangle with towers'; 'Enveloping arms with towers'; 'Arc with towers'; 'Flat arc with wings protruding from both sides of the line'. These technical terms denote of course the shape of the front-line according to the tactics used at each phase of the fighting and similar terms are known in other armies. The 'towers' for instance are explained in detail. They are fighting units organized in square formations moving forward. Their soldiers carry shields some three cubits long and spears eight cubits long; the shields are inscribed with the names of the angels. The shields of the first tower carried the name of Michael, of the second Gabriel, of the third Sariel, and the fourth Raphael—four towers in all.

The army did not consist of fighting units alone. There were corps of services too, such as 'camp prefects' whose age was from 50 to 60; 'provosts' whose age was from 40 to 50, and a group of other services, the age of whose soldiers was 25 to 30. These included 'those that spoil the slain', 'those who collect the booty', 'those who cleanse the land' (i.e. burial groups), 'those who guard the arms' and 'those who prepare the provisions'.

Obviously, the sect based its customs not only on the rules clearly specified in the Bible, but sometimes even on their interpretation of the implications of Biblical injunction. For example, on the subject of mobilization and service-exemption, the author gives this rule:

No young boy or woman shall enter their encampments when they go forth from Jerusalem to go to war and until they return. And anyone halt or blind or lame or a man in whose body there is permanent defect or a man affected by an impurity of his flesh, all these shall not go to war with them. All of them shall be volunteers for battle and sound in spirit and flesh and ready for the day of vengeance. And any man who is not pure with regard to his sexual organs on the day of battle shall not join them in battle for holy angels are in common with their hosts.

He also specifies the exact distance between the camp and the ablutions area: 'there shall be a space between all their camps and the place of the "hand" [latrine] about two thousand cubits, and no unseemly evil thing shall be seen in the vicinity of their camps.'

The scroll contains a detailed description of the duties of

the priests at the various stages of war, and the procedure of sacrificing at the Temple during the Sabbatical year: 'The chiefs of the priests they shall dispose after the Chief Priest and his deputy, twelve chiefs to be serving in the daily burnt offering before God.' The Priests are divided into twenty-six and not twenty-four courses as was common. This division stems from the fact that the sect followed a 364-day calendar, divided into fifty-two weeks. Heads of the courses serve according to a roster. After them in the service come the chiefs of the Levites, twelve in number, who serve 'continually . . . one to each tribe', and keep a definite order of priority amongst themselves. After them come the Chiefs of the Tribes and fathers of the congregation 'to stand perpetually in the Gates of the Temple', followed by the (lay) Israelites who will also serve 'on their festivals, on their new moons, and on the Sabbaths and on all days of the year'.

The major part of this scroll, however, deals with the different prayers to be said at the various stages of the war, and since the final battle on the last day of the war will be hard and bitter, and only on the 'seventh Lot' will the Sons of Light win their final victory, the prayers to be said must be appropriate to the action. There are prayers, of course, for the beginning of the battle; a prayer of special encouragement after the defeat of the Sons of Light; a curse of Belial and the Sons of Darkness after their defeat coupled with a prayer of gratitude and praise to God after the victory. Some paragraphs are devoted to the designation of the different priests who supervise the different prayers. Most are conducted by the Chief Priest himself. But some of the prayers and words of encouragement, particularly those that require movement along the front and among the fighting men, are supervised by a second priest detailed for that duty. The following translations of a few of the prayers may convey some idea of their quality, though it is not easy for a translation to capture the power and beauty of the original Hebrew. Here is part of what the Chief Priest says before setting out for battle:

For Thine is the war
And through the strength of Thy hand have their corpses been
    dashed to pieces with no one to bury them
And Goliath of Gath a mighty man of valour
Thou didst deliver into the hand of David Thy servant
Because he trusted in Thy great name
And not in sword and lance;
For the war is Thine.

He goes on to quote Isaiah in the same context:

From of old Thou hast announced to us the time appointed for
the mighty deed of Thy hand against the Kittim, saying 'then shall
Asshur fall with a sword not of man, and a sword not of man shall
devour him'.

And how beautiful is the next sentence:

For unto the hand of the poor Thou wilt deliver the enemies from
all lands and unto the hand of them that are prostrate in the dust
Thou wilt bring low all mighty men of the peoples.

This prayer ends with a request that God fight the battle of
the Sons of Light:

Arise oh mighty one
Take thy captives oh man of glory!
And take thy booty who dost valiantly
Lay thy hand in the neck of thine enemies,
And thy foot upon the bodies of the slain.
Crush the Gentiles thine opponents,
And let thy sword devour guilty flesh,
Fill thy land with glory
And thine inheritance with blessing,
Let there be a multitude of cattle in thy portions
Silver and gold and precious stones in thy palaces.
Oh Zion, rejoice exceedingly
And come forth in songs of joy oh Jerusalem
And be joyful all ye cities of Judah!
Open thy gates for ever
To let enter into thee the wealth of the Gentiles

And their kings shall serve thee
And all they that afflicted thee may bow down to thee
And the dust of thy feet they shall lick.
Oh daughters of my people, cry aloud with a voice of joy
Adorn yourselves with ornaments of glory
And rule over the kingdom of Kittim
And the Kingdom shall be God's
Over Israel shall be His eternal Dominion.

In the prayer of encouragement, following the defeat of the Sons of Light in one of the Lots, the Chief Priest says:

But ye, be strong and fear them not for they are destined for chaos, and their desire is for the [?] void, and their support as if it had not been. They did not know that from the God of Israel is all that is and that will be. And that He will annihilate Belial for all future times of eternity. Today is His appointed time to subdue and lay low the prince of the dominion of wickedness. And He will send eternal assistance—the might of an angel—to the Lot to be redeemed by Him. He has magnified the authority of Michael for eternal light, to light up in joy the House of Israel and peace and blessing to the Lot of God; so as to raise among the angels the authority of Michael and the dominion of Israel amongst all flesh.

After one of the defeats of the Sons of Darkness, when the Sons of Light are standing by their corpses, they have a special service of praise to God and curse to Belial in which they say:

Blessed be the God of Israel for all His holy thought and His true deeds; and blessed be all who served Him in righteousness, who know Him by faith. And cursed be Belial for the thought of hatred, and abhorred in his guilty authority; cursed be all spirits of his Lot for their wicked plan, and abhorred for all the works of their filthy uncleanness. For they are the Lot of Darkness, but the Lot of God is destined for light eternal.

Similarly, when they return from the battle field to their camps:

They shall bless, together, the God of Israel and exalt His name in joyful unison and shall solemnly declare: blessed be the God of Israel who preserveth mercy for His covenant and times ordained for salvation for the people to be redeemed by Him. And hath called them that stumble unto wondrous mighty deeds, and an assembly of nations He hath gathered in for annihilation without remnant, so as to raise up by judgement them whose heart has melted, and to open the mouth of the dumb to sing His mighty deeds, and to teach the weak-handed warfare. He giveth to them whose knees totter strength to stand, and strength of loins to the shoulder of them who have been brought low. Through the poor in spirit there shall be gnawed the hard heart, and through those whose way is undefiled shall all wicked nations come to an end, and all their mighty men shall not be able to resist.

The last part of the scroll is devoted to a description of the Seven Lots of the battle, and the victory of each Lot, with the alternating fortunes of the Sons of Light and the Sons of Darkness.

But in the seventh Lot, when the great hand of God shall be raised up against Belial and all the army of his dominion for eternal defeat and the Sons of Japhet shall fall never to rise again, and the Kittim shall be smashed to pieces without remnant and survival—there shall be an upraising of the hand of God against the whole multitude of Belial.

In the final victory of the Sons of Light, a great miracle occurs, like the one in Judah when Sennacherib besieged Jerusalem. They rise up in the morning 'and behold, they are all slain . . . for they have fallen there by the sword of God'. This may also be the reason why the author of the scroll names the enemies of Israel 'the Kittim of Asshur', since it is in the battle against them that the miracle prophesied in Isaiah will recur: 'Then shall Asshur fall with a sword not of man, and a sword not of man shall devour him.'

The War Scroll before unrolling

The first sheet of the War Scroll

The Commentary of Habakkuk

CHAPTER 16

The Scroll of the Apocryphal Genesis

THE FOUR SCROLLS bought from the Syrian Metropolitan, as we mentioned earlier, included one which was so fragile that its unrolling presented many severe problems. When that scroll reached America, a fragment of one of its first pages somehow became detached, and thus it was revealed that—unlike the other scrolls—it was written not in Hebrew but in Aramaic. John C. Trever, who perused the fragment, succeeded in deciphering on it the name of Lamech and that of his wife Bit (or Bat)-Enosh (i.e. the daughter of Enosh), who is also mentioned in the Book of Jubilees. Since this fragment quoted Lamech using first-person speech, Trever assumed that he had found 'the Apocryphal Book of Lamech, mentioned once in a Greek list of Apocryphal Books'. On the basis of this conclusion by Trever, the scroll has up to now been called the Lamech Scroll.

It will be recalled that the Syrian Metropolitan would not permit American scholars to unroll and publish the scroll until all four scrolls were purchased from him, and so no additional information about it could be gained at the time. However, as soon as the scroll was despatched to Israel, it was handed over to Professor Bieberkraut, who, under the supervision of the late Professor Sukenik, had worked on the unrolling of the first three scrolls six years earlier. The unrolling of the Lamech Scroll, this time under the direction of my colleague Dr N. Avigad and myself, was not at all easy. Even when it first reached the Americans, Professor Burrows said: 'Only very careful expert treatment can ever unroll enough to recover any considerable part of the text, if indeed this is possible at all.' However, patient and very laborious efforts finally bore fruit and some complete pages of the scroll have been saved.

The external and middle parts of the scroll were badly preserved. This was to be expected. But fortunately its inner part was well preserved, and, when opened, astonished us: the scroll was not the Lamech Scroll at all. Instead it was an Aramaic document related to the Book of Genesis, interwoven with various stories, most of them based on stories from Genesis, but with additional details and hitherto unknown names. The style and character of the stories are similar to those of the Book of Jubilees and some parts of the Book of Enoch—a fact which strengthens the opinion that the books of the sect belong to that literary category.

The last few inner pages of the scroll deal with Genesis xii, xiii, xiv, and xv. All are written in the first person by Abraham. Chapter xii has, among others, an interesting description of how Sarai (or Sara) was taken by the King of Egypt, and adds many absorbing details about Sara's beauty which are lacking in the Old Testament. These descriptions are based on the paragraph in Genesis which says: 'And it came to pass, that when Abram was come into Egypt the Egyptians beheld the woman that she was very fair. The Princes also of Pharaoh saw her, and commended her before Pharaoh: and the woman was taken into Pharaoh's house.'

The following is the full translation of the description of Sara's beauty, as related to the Pharaoh by his chief prince Horkanosh, as well as of the events which followed, described by Abraham:

...... 'How ... and (how) beautiful the look of her face ... and how ...... fine is the hair of her head, how fair indeed are her eyes and how pleasing her nose and all the radiance of her face ... how beautiful her breast and how lovely all her whiteness. Her arms goodly to look upon, and her hands how perfect ... all the appearance of her hands. How fair her palms and how long and fine all the fingers of her hands. Her legs how beautiful and how without blemish her thighs. And all maidens and all brides that go beneath the wedding canopy are not more fair than she. And above all women is she lovely and higher is her beauty than that of them all, and with all her beauty there is much wisdom in her. And the tip of her hands is comely.'

And when the King heard the words of Horkanosh and the words of his two companions, for all three spoke as one man, he desired her exceedingly and he sent at once to bring her to him and he looked upon her and marvelled at all her loveliness and took her to him to wife and sought to slay me. And Sarai spoke to the King, saying, 'He is my brother,' that it might be well with me (that I might profit thereby). And I, Abram, was saved because of her and was not slain. And I wept, I, Abram, with grievous weeping, I and with me, Lot, my brother's son, wept that night when Sarai was taken from me by force.

That night I prayed and entreated and begged and said in sorrow, as my tears fell, 'Blessed art Thou, Most High God, Lord of all worlds, because Thou art Lord and Master of all and ruler of all the kings of earth, all of whom Thou judgest. Behold now I cry before Thee, my Lord, against Pharaoh-Zoan, King of Egypt, because my wife has been taken from me by force. Do Thou judge him for me and let me behold Thy mighty hand descend upon him and all his household and may he not this night defile my wife. And men shall know, my Lord, that Thou art the Lord of all the kings of earth.' And I wept and grieved.

That night the Most High God sent a pestilential wind to afflict him and all his household, a wind that was evil. And it smote him and all his house and he could not come near her nor did he know her and he was with her two years. And at the end of two years the plagues and the afflictions became grievous and strong in him and in all his house. And he sent and called for all the wise men of Egypt and all the wizards and all the physicians of Egypt, if perchance they might heal him from that pestilence, him and his house. And all the physicians and wizards and wise men could not rise up to heal him, for the wind smote them all and they fled.

Then came to me Horkanosh and besought me to come and to pray for the King and to lay my hands upon him that he might live, for in the dream. . . . And Lot said unto him, 'Abram, my

146

uncle, cannot pray for the King while Sarai, his wife, is with him. Go now and tell the King to send away his wife to her husband and he will pray for him and he will live.'

And when Horkanosh heard these words of Lot he went and said to the King, 'All these plagues and afflictions with which my lord, the King, is plagued and afflicted, are for the sake of Sarai, the wife of Abram. Restore her, Sarai, to Abram, her husband, and the plague will depart from thee and the evil will pass away.'

And he called me to him and said to me, 'What hast thou done unto me for the sake of [Sara]i, that thou hast told me "She is my sister", and she is indeed thy wife, and I took her to me to wife. Behold thy wife who is with me, go thy way and depart from all the land of Egypt. And now pray for me and all my house that this evil wind may depart from us.'

And I prayed for . . . this swiftly [?] and I laid my hand upon his head and the plague departed from him and the evil [wind] was gone and he lived. And the King rose and said unto me . . . . and the King swore to me with an oath that cannot [be changed . . .] . . . And the King gave him a large . . . . and much clothing of fine linen and purple . . . . . . before her, and also Hagar . . . and appointed men for me who would take [me] out. . . .

And I, Abram, went forth, exceedingly rich in cattle and also in silver and in gold, and I went up out [of Egypt and Lot], the son of my brother, with me. And Lot also had great possessions and took unto himself a wife from . . .

The scroll is unique also in preserving an original legend explaining why Abraham counselled Sara to hide her true identity. The explanation is in a dream that Abraham dreamed, of a cedar and a palm. Abraham wakes, tells Sara about the dream that frightened him and interprets its meaning to her: when they reach Egypt, there will be an attempt to kill him, but Sara will be able to save him. Thus, according to this legend, this deception was God's counsel, rather than Abraham's, revealed to the latter through a dream. The following is the story as told by Abraham:

. . . Now we passed through our land and entered into the land of the sons of Ham, the land of Egypt. And I, Abram, dreamed a dream on the night of our entering into the land of Egypt and lo! I saw in my dream one cedar tree and one palm . . . . And men came and sought to cut down and uproot the cedar and to leave the palm by itself. And the palm cried out and said, 'Cut not down the cedar, for cursed is he who will fell . . .' And for the sake of the palm the cedar was saved. And no . . .

And I woke from my slumber that night and I said to Sarai, my wife, 'A dream have I dreamt . . . and I am frightened by this dream.' And she said to me, 'Tell me thy dream that I may know.' And I began to tell her that dream.

'. . . the dream . . . that they will seek to slay me and to save thee alive. This day all the good . . . . that he is my brother and I shall live because of thee and my soul shall be saved for thy sake . . . from me and to kill me.' And Sarai wept at my words that night . . .

The paragraph in Genesis xiii. 13, describing Lot's parting with Abraham, gets very short treatment in the scroll's parallel version. On the other hand the scroll gives more details of the paragraph concerning God's words to Abraham:

And the Lord said unto Abram after that Lot was separated from him, lift up now thine eyes, and look from the place where thou art northward, and southward, and eastward and westward. For all the land which thou seest, to thee will I give it, and to thy seed for ever. And I will make thy seed as the dust of the earth: so that if a man can number the dust of the earth, then shall thy seed also be numbered. Arise, walk through the land in the length of it and in the breadth of it; for I will give it unto thee. Then Abram removed his tent, and came and dwelt in the plain of Mamre, which is in Hebron, and built there an altar unto the Lord.

Abraham in the corresponding passage in the scroll describes in detail how he walked the length and breadth of the country and enumerates the names of places he had passed. These names are interesting topographically, as they resemble the names in the Book of Jubilees, but in some details they add new material.

In reading the following translation, the reader should note that instead of the traditional text: 'and look from the place where thou art,' the scroll reads: 'Get thee up to the Height of Hazor that is to the left of Beth-el, *the place where thou now dwellest*.' The author of the scroll apparently knew that the mountain east of Beth-el (913 metres) is not the highest in the vicinity; accordingly, he moved Abraham to a higher point, north of Beth-el, the Height of Hazor. The description of its location and character indicates clearly that it was an especially high place from which it was possible to see great distances: it may, therefore, be definitely concluded that the high place in question was Baal Hazor (2 Sam. xiii. 23), identified by most scholars with Gebel el-'Asur, eight kilometres north-east of Beth-el as the crow flies. This is the highest spot in central Palestine (1,003 metres) and it is unique in affording a view of both the Trans-Jordan, the Mediterranean and the hills of Hebron. The following is the translation of Abraham's description of the vision and his subsequent journey.

After this day Lot parted from me because of the deeds of our herdmen and he went forth and dwelt in the valley of the Jordan and all his possessions were with him. And I also increased greatly that which he had and he herded his flocks and reached even to Sodom. And he built himself a house in Sodom and dwelt in it. And I dwelt on the mount of Beth-el and I was grieved that Lot, the son of my brother, had parted from me.

And God appeared to me in a vision of the night and He spoke to me, saying, 'Get thee up to Ramath-Hazor (Height of Hazor) that is to the left of Beth-el, the place where thou now dwellest, and lift up thine eyes and look eastward and westward and southward and northward and behold all this land that I give to thee and to thy seed forever.' And I went up on the morrow to Ramath-Hazor and I beheld the land from that high place, from the River of Egypt to Lebanon and Shenir and from the Great Sea to Hauran and all the land of Gebal unto Kadesh and all the Great Wilderness east of Hauran and Shenir unto Euphrates. And He said to me, 'To thy seed will I give all this land and they shall inherit it forever. And I will multiply thy seed as the dust of the earth which no man can number, nor shall thy seed be numbered. Arise, walk through the land, go forth and see how much is its length and its breadth, for I will give it unto thee and unto thy seed for ever.'

And I, Abram, went forth to journey about the land and to look upon it. And I began to wander from the River Gihon and I came to the shore of the sea until I reached the Mount of the Ox. And I journeyed from the shore of this Great Salt Sea and I went along the Mount of the Ox eastward in the breadth of the land, till I reached the Red Sea and I went on along the Red Sea till I reached the Tongue of the Sea of Reeds that goes out from the Red Sea and I turned southward till I came to the River Gihon.

And I returned and came in peace to my home. And I found all my household in peace and I went and I dwelt at the Oaks of Mamre which is in Hebron, northeast of Hebron. And I built there an altar and offered upon it a burnt offering and a meat offering to the Most High God and I ate and I drank there, I and all my house. And I sent and called for Mamre and 'Anaram and Eshcol, the three Amorite brothers, my friends, and they ate together with me and they drank with me.

Chapter xiv of Genesis deals with the war of the four kings, Amraphel, Arioch, Chedorlaomer and Tidal, against the five kings: Bera, King of Sodom, Birsha, King of Gomorrah, Shinab, King of Admah, Shemeber, King of Zeboiim, and the King of Bela. The version of this chapter in the scroll enriches our knowledge of place-names, some of which were unknown up to now. On the other hand the second part of the same chapter, which deals with Lot's captivity and how Abram sent his servants to redeem him, is almost identical with the Genesis story, except for a few topographical details.

Before these days there came Chedorlaomer, king of Elam, Amraphel, king of Babylon, Arioch, king of Cappadocia (Kapatok), Tidal, king of nations who is between the Rivers, and they made war upon Bera, king of Sodom, and upon Birsha, king of Gomorrah ('Amoram), and Shinab, king of Admah, and Shem'abad [*sic*] of Zeboiim, and the king of Bela. All these were joined together for war in the vale of Siddim.

And the king of Elam and the kings that were with him prevailed over the king of Sodom and all his confederates and they levied a tribute upon them. Twelve years they paid their tribute to the king of Elam and in the thirteenth year they rebelled against him. And in the fourteenth year the king of Elam led all his confederates and they went up by the Way of the Wilderness, and they kept smiting and taking spoil all the way from the River Euphrates, and they smote the Rephaim who were in Ashteroth Karnaim and the Zamzumim who were in Ammon and the Emim who were in Shaveh Hagiryoth and the Horites who were in the mountains of Gebal, until they came to El-paran which is by the wilderness. And they returned . . . in Hazezon-tamar.

And there went out against them the king of Sodom and the king [of Gomorrah and the king] of Admah and the king of Zeboiim and the king of Bela and they [joined] battle in the vale of Siddim with Chedorla[omer, the king of Elam and the kings] who were with him. And the king of Sodom was defeated and he fled and the king of Gomorrah fell into the pits . . . and the king of Elam (took) all the goods of Sodom [and Gomorrah . . .] and they took Lot, the son of the brother of Abram who dwelt in Sodom together with them and all his goods.

And there came one of the herdmen of the cattle that Abram had given to Lot, one that had escaped from captivity to Abram. And Abram then dwelt in Hebron. And (the herdman) told him that Lot, his brother's son, was taken captive and all his goods, but he was not slain, and that the kings had gone on by the way of the Great Valley to their land and that they were taking captives and booty, and smiting and slaying and making their way to the province of Damascus.

And Abram wept for Lot, his brother's son, and Abram grew strong and rose up and chose from among his servants men trained for war, three hundred and eighteen. And 'Anaram and Eshcol and Mamre went with him. And he pursued them till he reached Dan and found them encamped in the Vale of Dan and he fell upon them by night from all their four quarters. And he kept slaying them in the night and he vanquished them and he pursued them and all of them fled before him till they reached

Helbon which is set at the left hand of Damascus. And he rescued from them all that they had taken captive and all they had taken as booty and all their goods. And he also rescued Lot, his brother's son, and all his goods and all the captives they had taken he brought back.

And the king of Sodom heard that Abram brought back all the captives and all the spoils, and he went up towards him and came to Salem that is Jerusalem. And Abram was pitched in the valley of Shaveh which is the king's dale, the Plain of Beth ha-Kerem. And Melchizedek, king of Salem, brought forth food and drink to Abram and all the men that were with him. And he was a priest of the Most High God and he blest Abram and he said, 'Blessed be Abram of the Most High God, Lord of heaven and earth, and blessed be the Most High God which hath delivered thine enemies into thy hand.' And he gave him a tithe of all the goods of the king of Elam and his companions.

Then the king of Sodom drew near and said to Abram, 'My lord Abram, give me the souls that are mine, who are captives with thee, whom thou hast rescued from the king of Elam. And the spoils all of them shall be left to thee.'

Then said Abram to the king of Sodom, 'I lift up mine hand today unto the Most High God, lord of heaven and earth, that from a thread even to a shoe latchet will I not take aught that is thine, lest thou shouldst say, "From my goods cometh all the wealth of Abram." Save only that which the young men that are with me have already eaten and save the portion of the three men that went with me. They are masters of their share to give it to thee.'

And Abram restored all the goods and all the captives and gave them to the king of Sodom. And all the captives that were with him from this land he set free and sent them all away.

Chapter xv, in which Abram asks God to give him a son and heir as he is childless, is only partly preserved; but even that part has a few interesting additions in comparison with the Biblical narrative.

We thus learn that far from being the Lamech Scroll, this is an Apocryphal version of Genesis with additional stories similar to some books of the Apocrypha, written in apocalyptic style and told in the first person singular. The part which mentions Lamech corresponds to Genesis v, except that it is more concerned with a description of the birth of Lamech's son, Noah, and bears a strong similarity to what is written about this in the Book of Enoch.

The great interest, however, lies in the additional material. From the Book of Enoch we knew of the following legend concerning the birth of Noah:

And after some days my son Methuselah took a wife for his son Lamech, and she became pregnant by him and bore a son. And his body was white as snow and red as the blooming of a rose, and the hair of his head and his long locks were white as wool and his eyes beautiful. And when he opened his eyes, he lighted up the whole house like the sun, and the whole house was very bright. And thereupon he arose in the hands of the midwife, opened his mouth, and conversed with the Lord of righteousness. And his father Lamech was afraid of him and fled, and came to his father Methuselah. And he said unto him: 'I have begotten a strange son, diverse from and unlike man, and resembling the sons of God of heaven, and his nature is different and he is not like us, and his eyes are as the rays of the sun, and his countenance is glorious. And it seems to me that he is not sprung from me but from the angels, and I fear that in his days a wonder may be wrought on the earth. And now, my father, I am here to petition thee and implore thee that thou mayst go to Enoch, our father, and learn from him the truth, for his dwelling-place is amongst the angels.' And when Methuselah heard the words of his son, he came to me to the ends of the earth, for he had heard that I was there, and he cried aloud, and I heard his voice and I came to him. And I said unto him: 'Behold, here am I, my son, wherefore hast thou come to me?' And he answered and said: 'Because of a great cause of anxiety have I come to thee, and because of a disturbing vision have I approached. And now, my father hear me: Unto Lamech, my son, there hath been born a son, the like of whom there is none, and his nature is not like man's nature, and the colour of his body is whiter than snow and redder than the bloom of a rose, and the hair of his head is whiter than white wool, and his eyes are like the rays of the sun, and he opened his eyes and thereupon

153

lighted up the whole house. And he arose in the hands of the mid-wife, and opened his mouth and blessed the Lord of heaven. And his father Lamech became afraid and fled to me, and did not believe that he was sprung from him, but that he was in the like-ness of the angels of heaven: and behold I have come to thee that thou make known to me the truth.'

The scroll, however, preserves a very intimate dialogue be-tween Lamech and his wife Bat-Enosh. After relating the events which took place on Noah's birth, the author tells us that Lamech was perplexed; but—and this is interesting—before going to ask for the advice of his father Methuselah, he, quite naturally, approaches his wife and cross-questions her. The following translation is the exact rendering of this unique version, incomplete as it is as a result of the decay of the leather:

Then I thought in my heart that the conception had been from the Watchers and the . . . from the holy ones or [?] the fallen angels. And my heart was changed because of this child.

Then I, Lamech, was frightened and I came to Bat-Enosh, my wife, and [I said] . . . '[. . . Swear to me] by the Most High, the Lord of greatness, King of all worlds . . . . Sons of Heaven till thou tellest me all in truth if . . . . . . [In truth?] tell me without lies . . . . . . By the King of all worlds till thou speakest with me in truth and with no lies' . . . . . .

Then Bat-Enosh, my wife, spoke to me with vigour and with . . . . . . And she said, 'O my brother and O my lord, remember my pleasure . . . . the period, and my spirit into the midst of its sheath and I in truth all . . . .' . . . . . . And my heart then had changed within me greatly.

When Bat-Enosh, my wife, perceived that my countenance had changed . . . Then she suppressed her wrath and spoke to me and said, 'O my lord and O my [brother] . . . . . . My pleasure. I swear to thee by the great Holy One, the King of H[eaven?] . . . that thine is this seed and from thee is this conception and from thee was the fruit formed . . . . . . And it is no stranger's, nor is it of any of the Watchers or of the Sons of Heaven . . . [What] has so altered and blemished thy countenance and [why] is thy spirit so low? . . . In truth I speak with thee.'

Then I, Lamech, hastened to Methuselah, my father, and I [told him] all . . . his father and he would of a surety learn all from him, for he was the beloved and [. . . with angels] his lot was apportioned and to him they tell all. And when Methuselah heard . . . . to Enoch, his father, to learn all in truth from him. . . . his will. And he went to . . . . . . and found him there. . . . .

And he said to Enoch, his father, 'O my father and O my lord, to whom I . . . . And I shall tell thee that thou shouldst not be angered that I have come hither . . . . . . Fear. . . . .'

The missing pages of this scroll, or those which have not yet been completely deciphered, most probably dealt with the material of Genesis chapters vi-xi; and it may be assumed that those sheets which have not been discovered contained the remaining chapters from xv onwards. It would thus be reasonable to call this scroll: 'A Genesis Apocryphon'.

The particular importance of the scroll is that it is the only one of the seven whole scrolls discovered which is written in Aramaic, and this gives us a Biblical document of the literature written during the last centuries before the destruction of the Temple.

Dr Avigad and I have just published a book dealing with five columns of this scroll, and we hope that the entire decipherment will be completed in the near future.[1]

[1] N. Avigad and Y. Yadin: *A Genesis Apocryphon*, The Hebrew University Press, Jerusalem, 1956.

CHAPTER 17

The Copper Scrolls—The Scrolls of Treasures

IT WOULD be unfair to sum up our discussion of the seven scrolls without adding a few words about the Copper Scroll, which when opened revealed contents of a most exciting and stimulating nature.

As described earlier, the two copper scrolls were discovered in 1952 in Cave 3. But owing to their delicate state, the result of the oxidization of the metal, it took a long time before a safe method of unrolling them could be devised. There was much speculation and conjecture by scholars about their contents, with a free use of fertile imagination. It was only a year after their discovery that the German scholar Professor Kuhn, who happened to visit the Rockefeller Museum in Jerusalem, succeeded in deciphering a few words which protruded on the outside fragments of the scrolls—in 'negative' of course. Since these scrolls were made of metal, their writing was not in ink, but was beaten out with the aid of a sharp instrument. The few words that were thus deciphered naturally aroused the wonder of the scholarly world. In order that the reader may savour some of the excitement caused by those words, they are quoted in full:

Fragment A
    Line 5: . . . four . . .
    Line 6: . . . cubits . . .
    Line 7: . . . four hundred . . .
    Line 8: . . . the second dig six cubits . . .
    Line 12: . . . from this side dig seven cubits . . .
    Line 14: . . . dig six cubits until the . . .

Fragment B
  Line 1: . . . the house . . .
  Line 5: . . . dig seven cubits . . .

Fragment C:
  Line 4: . . . on this side . . .
  Line 5: . . . eight cubits . . .
  Line 6: . . . and a half.

Fragment D:
  Line 2: . . . from above . . .
  Line 6: . . . all . . .
  Line 10: . . . the opening . . .
  Line 11: . . . gold . . .

This discovery was naturally followed by a fresh wave of conjectures: a list of hidden treasures, plans of important buildings, and so on. The actual content of these scrolls was only brought to light as late as the summer of 1955, when some English scholars persuaded the Jordanian Government to let them bring the scrolls to Manchester for treatment by Professor Wright-Baker, Professor of Mechanical Engineering at the Manchester College of Technology. Professor Wright-Baker eventually succeeded in opening the scrolls. Owing to corrosion of the metal it was impossible to unroll the scrolls as we had the leather ones; he therefore sawed them into strips. The process was divided into four stages. First the scrolls were mounted in a way which enabled treatment without direct and unnecessary handling. All dust was removed from the centre of the scroll and a spindle inserted through the hollow and tightened with dental plaster. Next the roll was coated with a chemical solution to strengthen the decomposed metal. Then the actual cutting was done, with the aid of a specially designed sawing machine with a highly sensitive control. The machine cut the scroll into strips and finally the severed sections were separately removed.

The saw was $1\frac{3}{4}$ inches in diameter and $0\cdot006$ inches wide. It could be moved along the surface of the scroll by the lightest touch. The cutting of each section lasted between two and ten minutes. In several cases it was even possible to cut between the columns of the letters. Professor Wright-Baker controlled the cutting with the aid of a magnifying glass. After the cutting, dust was removed from the segments and the letters showed up quite clearly. When the job was done, the following facts were established: originally the two rolls belonged to one plaque, 0·03 inches thick and composed of three parts nailed together. Its overall length was eight feet, and its width some eleven inches. After it had been rolled— probably in great haste—it must have split into two parts to form the two scrolls found in the cave. Professor Wright-Baker says that there is no indication whatsoever that the scrolls were meant to be hung on a wall. Originally the scroll contained some three thousand letters, and according to Professor Wright-Baker only about one hundred and fifty had been lost through early breakages.

The full contents of this scroll have not so far been published, but from the official communiqués and from information from various sources, it appears that the scroll contains a long list of hiding places of treasures to the amount of some six thousand gold and silver talents. Assuming that the weight of a talent in those days was about twenty-four kilos, some idea may be gleaned of the value of the treasures. The list mentions some sixty places spread all over Palestine, from Hebron in the south to Mount Gerizim in the north, and possibly even further north. Most of the places are centred round Jerusalem, mainly around the Temple and the Kidron Valley. According to the scroll, the treasures were hidden in wells, in tombs and near conspicuous objects, such as trees and springs.

The descriptions of the localities of the caches are almost standard. First a place name in Palestine is given. Then come details describing a geographical or topographical object. Thirdly, the depth of the treasure below the surface is recorded in cubits. Finally come the details of the treasure itself.

Only the following descriptions have so far been published:

1. In the cistern which is below the rampart, on the east side, in a place hollowed out of the rock, six hundred bars of silver.
2. In the pit nearby, towards the north, near the graves, in a hole opening towards the north, there is a copy of this book with explanations, measurements and all details.
3. Close by, below the southern corner of the porticoes, at Zadok's tomb, and underneath the pilaster in the exedras: a vessel of incense in artemisia wood and a vessel of incense in cassia wood.

Similarly, there are more details about other treasures, such as nine hundred talents, sixteen talents, two jars full of silver, and so forth, each case giving details of the place of hiding, the outstanding landmark, the depth to dig, and the kind of treasure.

We cannot yet know with certainty what those treasures mean or by whom they were hidden. Some scholars believe the list to be imaginary; others believe it to be a list of the Temple's treasures, hidden about the time of the siege. Until the scroll is fully published it would be rash to jump to conclusions. But it is not excluded that here we have a list of the treasures of the sect, a list hidden by one of its members, possibly the treasurer, before their escape, and beaten into a copper sheet in the hope of finding it on their eventual return.

However, even if it is found that the list is wholly imaginary and was compiled solely to serve some special religious purpose, it still remains of high importance, and with its full publication we may expect many surprises, both linguistic and topographical.

CHAPTER 18

The Date of the Scrolls and the Identification of the Sect

HAVING examined the most important scrolls from the Dead Sea, we are now in a position to deal with two main questions:

1. Who were the people who compiled these books?
2. When did they live?

From the moment of discovery and the first publications, scholars have been engaged in vehement argument over their date and the identity of their compilers. The most extreme opinion in that field was voiced by Professor Zeitlin, who claimed the scrolls to be of very late date. As long as the exact location of their initial discovery remained unknown (since the first ones, as the reader will recall, were bought both by Sukenik and the Metropolitan through antiquities dealers), such an argument may have been tenable. Today, however, Zeitlin and his followers are an extreme minority among scholars, for the archaeological excavations conducted in the neighbourhood of Qumran have completely demolished that theory. The caves excavated have revealed many fragments of other scrolls, and even in the first cave itself—in which the seven scrolls were discovered—archaeologists have found fragments, some of which fit like a jig-saw puzzle into missing parts of the scrolls. Excavations in the ruins of Qumran also yielded many jars of the same type as the jars that housed the first scrolls. So that Zeitlin's arguments no longer have any archaeological basis. However, most of the scholars who believe in the antiquity of the scrolls are still divided as to their exact date—but here they differ within the limits of a couple of hundred years.

In order to clarify the date of the scrolls we must distinguish between three completely separate facts:

1. The date of the compilation of the text.
2. The date of the copies now in our possession.
3. The date they were hidden in the caves.

Let us for a moment imagine a modern library destroyed during the last war by aerial bombardment. We might find in it books compiled at different periods, which were received by the library at different periods. If, however, we succeeded in establishing the exact date of the destruction of the library, we should at least know the latest date to which its contents may be attributed.

Let us therefore begin with the last question: when, at the latest, were the scrolls stored in the Qumran caves? Most scholars agree today that it was not later than AD 70, the date of the destruction by the Romans of the Second Jewish Temple in Jerusalem. The detailed evidence for that assumption has already been given, and the archaeological finds in the ruins of Qumran have been described in detail. But to sum up, the reader may remember that many coins of the first century BC and the early part of the first century AD were found among the ruins. Moreover, it can be logically assumed that during the cruel war which followed the revolt against the Romans the people who lived near the Dead Sea were not spared, but were in fact driven from there or exterminated by the Roman army, and that before the Romans arrived they managed to hide their books in the caves. Another proof is the jars found in the ruins. Though scholars cannot exactly determine their date, all are agreed that they are not later than AD 70. Moreover, I have mentioned that some of the scrolls were found wrapped in linen kerchiefs. Parts of these kerchiefs were sent to Professor W. F. Libby in the United States in 1949 for examination through the Carbon 14 process. He established that, according to the energy lost by the linen flax from which they were woven since they ceased to 'live', these kerchiefs were some 1,917 years old, plus or minus two hundred years. Unfortunately the Carbon 14 test cannot yet be more accurate than that. In other words we can assume that the wrappers were woven 2,117 years ago at the earliest, that is during the first half of the second century BC, and 1,717 years ago at the latest, that is during the first half of the third century AD. Although this date may not be very exact, it is still quite important since it confirms the date arrived at by scholars through other means, and completely negates the opinion of those who claim the scrolls to be Medieval or forged. In short, the answer to our first question is that most probably the scrolls were stored away about AD 70.

As for the second question, when were the scrolls now in our possession copied, we must refer mainly to palaeographical research. We must examine their writing. Here, too, it is logical to assume that the scrolls were not all copied at the same time. On the contrary, some of them, such as the complete Isaiah Scroll, seem to have been used by the sect for a long period before being stored, judging by the many later amendments and the general wear and tear. Unfortunately, however, the palaeographical data from the end of the Second Jewish Temple is not abundant, and has not yet reached a stage of accuracy that would enable us to fix within a few years the date of each scroll. In fact, until the discovery of these scrolls, we had hardly any manuscripts which could be dated with certainty to that period. But there is the striking resemblance between the writing of the scrolls in general and that found on inscriptions on ossuaries and tombstones which are known to date back to the end of the Second Temple; this undoubtedly indicates that the style of the writing can be ascribed to the first century BC or the first half of the first century AD.

We are now left with the last problem of the date of the

scrolls, the date, that is, of their compilation or author-ship.

It is self-evident that the different scrolls were compiled at different times. The Book of Isaiah, as we know, was written several hundred years earlier, and this applies to all the other Biblical books which have been discovered among the scrolls. We must, therefore, when discussing this problem, approach each scroll individually, and the common means to establish its date is to try and find in its contents some connexion with known historic–archaeological facts.

Let us start with the Commentary on Habakkuk, which is replete with hints of historical events and figures. We have already noted, in discussing this scroll, that the author of the Habakkuk Commentary was engrossed with two different problems; that of the cruel foe coming from outside the boundaries of Israel, the Kittim; and that of the persecution of the members of the sect and especially their leader, the Teacher of Righteousness, by the Wicked Priest. If we were able to identify the Kittim, the Teacher of Righteousness and the Wicked Priest, we should probably be in a position to establish the date of writing of the scroll. But this is more difficult than it seems, since there is more than one plausible theory on the identification of all three.

For the writer of the Commentary the Chaldeans mentioned in Habakkuk's prophecy are the Kittim of his own day. These Kittim, like the Chaldeans of Habakkuk, are a mighty people coming from afar with horses and frightening all nations. They overrun the fortresses of the people, conquer and destroy them, take much booty, are very cruel and show no pity even to infants, children, women, and the aged. Their rulers change frequently, and each comes, one after the other, to destroy the land. Moreover, 'they sacrifice to their standards and their weapons of war are their object of worship'. And finally, in the end 'the last priests of Jerusalem' will be given 'into the hand of the army of the Kittim'.

Who then, were these Kittim? In Genesis x. 4, we find
'The sons of Javan, Elisha, and Tarshish, Kittim, and
Dodanim'. Many other Biblical books mention them too in
a general or particular reference to the peoples around the
shores of the Mediterranean. Most of these references were
interpreted by the Septuagint and the Vulgate as referring to
the Romans. Josephus, for example, says that in his times the
Hebrews call most islanders and all dwellers of the Mediterranean shores, 'Kittim'. On the other hand, we find in the
Book of Maccabees that Alexander came from the land of
Kittim ('Alexander the Son of Philipos the Macedonian who
came from the land of Kittim'). Thus, according to the use of
the name Kittim by the Jews during the period of the Second
Temple, one can say with certainty that it referred to both the
Greek and Roman nations, depending on the period of the
respective scroll. This of course does not help us to solve the
final problem; who are they, Greek or Roman? As far as the
Commentary of Habakkuk is concerned, there is great significance in the fact that they seem to have 'worshipped their
standards'. The eminent French scholar, Dupont-Sommer,
was the first to suggest the identification of the Kittim in
Habakkuk with the Romans, since the cult of the Signa was
typical of the Romans and the Romans alone. This is a most
brilliant theory, and even scholars who think differently have
not yet successfully refuted it. On the other hand, however,
since the Kittim in Habakkuk are always referred to in a
future tense, 'they will come', some scholars tend to believe
that the book was written before the Roman conquest but
close to it, when their imminent approach was already generally felt in the country.

Now, however, we have the Nahum Commentary which
provides a clear solution to the problem of identification of
the Kittim, in the passage: 'Kings of Greece from Antichos
until the appearance of the rulers of the Kittim.' Without yet
trying to verify the identification of Antichos, we can see that
the sentence differentiates clearly between 'the Kings of

Greece' as referring to the Seleucid kings, the successors of Alexander in Syria, and the Kittim who replace them, namely the Romans. Here, too, as with the Habakkuk Commentary, the author uses the term 'Kittite Rulers' to indicate the first Kittite rulers as distinct from the Greek kings. We can therefore say now with some confidence that the Kittim, as referred to in the writings of the sect, are the Romans, destined to succeed the Greek kings. The style of the sentence seems to indicate that the commentary was written before the Romans took possession of the Orient, though at a time when it was already clear that this was about to happen. On the other hand the interpretation is also possible, as with the other apocalyptic books, that it may have been written after the Roman occupation.

We shall later return to the problem of the Kittim when discussing the date of the scroll of the War of the Sons of Light against the Sons of Darkness, in which they play a prominent part.

As to the Wicked Priest and the Teacher of Righteousness, the problem is still more complicated. For the descriptions referring to the Wicked Priest in the scrolls are very cursory and offer very little data for definite identification. Indeed, information on this point is so meagre that there is hardly a priest from the times of the Second Temple who has not been identified with the Wicked Priest of the scrolls by some scholar or other. Each scholar has his own theory. Some think the Kittim to be Greeks and therefore identify the Wicked Priest with known priests of the third century, the second century and the beginning of the first century BC. Those who believe the Kittim to be Romans naturally make the Wicked Priest one of the priests of the end of the Hasmonean era or the period following the Roman conquest.

The only things, therefore, that can be said with certainty about the Wicked Priest are those which stem from what is written about him in the scroll itself:

The Wicked Priest who was called by the name of truth when he first took office, but when he ruled over Israel his heart was lifted up and he abandoned God and betrayed the statutes for the sake of wealth; and he stole and assembled the wealth of men of violence who had revolted against God; and he took the wealth of peoples thus adding upon himself the guilt of transgression; and ways of abominations he wrought in all impurity of uncleanness.

Or:

The Wicked Priest, whom because of the wrong done to the Teacher of Righteousness, and the men of his party, God delivered him into the hands of his enemies to torment him with smiting that he might be destroyed in bitterness of soul, for the evil he had done to His elect ones,

meaning that the end of the Wicked Priest was persecution by his enemies. But the main feature seems to have been the persecution of the Teacher of Righteousness by the Wicked Priest. From several hints in the Commentary on the Book of Psalms, it is possible to infer that the Wicked Priest killed, or at least tried to kill, the Teacher of Rignteousness; for example Psalms xxxvii, 32: 'The wicked watcheth the righteous, and seeketh to slay him' is interpreted by the writer as referring to 'The Wicked Priest who . . . . to kill him.'

There is, to sum up, as yet no means of identifying the Wicked Priest with certainty. Possibly some scholars may be justified in believing him to be the Hasmonean King, Alexander Jannaeus, who was well known for his cruelty and persecution of the different Jewish sects who opposed him. Even the descriptions of his later punishment and suffering fit this theory. And here the Commentary on Nahum throws surprising and significant light on that problem. The hero of the Commentary is named The Lion of Wrath, since the passage interprets the words of Nahum who mentions in chapter ii, 'lions', 'young lions' and 'lionesses'. 'The Lion of Wrath' emerges, as we have seen, as a most cruel character, who 'hangs men alive'. That description too, fits Alexander Jannaeus, (as do the descriptions of the Wicked Priest in the Habakkuk Commentary), and if it is possible to prove that 'the Lion of Wrath' and 'the Wicked Priest' are one and the same person, their identification, it seems, will have been established. The description of the cruelty of the 'Lion of Wrath' who hangs people alive, as referring to Jannaeus, is further strengthened by the previous passage in the same Commentary which mentions an historical character, who, with the aid of Josephus, can be perhaps identified. I refer to the passage: '[Deme]tris, King of Greece, who sought to enter Jerusalem by the counsel of the Seekers-after-Smooth-Things' (line 2). There seem to be good reasons to believe that the said Demetris is none other than Demetrius III, Eucerus, the Seleucid King of Syria, who was asked by the rebels to enter the country and fight with them against Jannaeus. The description of the rebellion against Jannaeus, the intervention of Demetrius and Jannaeus' later revenge—as told by Josephus—are so reminiscent of what is said in the Commentaries that it may be helpful to quote them as they are, from Josephus' book on *The Wars of the Jews*:

However, when he fought with Obodas, king of the Arabians, who had laid an ambush for him near Golan, and a plot against him, he lost his entire army, which was crowded together in a deep valley, and broken to pieces by the multitude of camels; and when he had made his escape to Jerusalem, he provoked the multitude, who hated him before, to make an insurrection against him, and this on account of the greatness of the calamity that he was under. However, he was then too hard for them; and in the several battles that were fought on both sides, he slew not fewer than fifty thousand of the Jews, in the interval of six years. Yet had he no reason to rejoice in these victories, since he did but consume his own kingdom; till at length he left off fighting, and endeavoured to come to a composition with them, by talking with his subjects; but this mutability and irregularity of his conduct made them hate him still more; and when he asked them why they so hated him, and what he should do, in order to appease them, they said, by killing himself; for that it would be then all they could do, to be reconciled to him who had done such tragical things to them, even when he was dead. At the same time they invited Demetrius, who was called Eucerus, to assist them; and as he readily complied with their request, in hopes of great advantages, and came with his army, the Jews joined with those their auxiliaries about Shechem.

Yet did Alexander meet both these forces with one thousand horsemen, and eight thousand mercenaries that were on foot. He had also with him that part of the Jews which favoured him, to the number of ten thousand; while the adverse party had three thousand horsemen, and fourteen thousand footmen. Now, before they joined battle, the kings made proclamation, and endeavoured to draw off each other's soldiers, and make them revolt; while Demetrius hoped to induce Alexander's mercenaries to leave him,— and Alexander hoped to induce the Jews that were with Demetrius to leave him; but, since neither the Jews would leave off their rage, nor the Greeks prove unfaithful, they came to an engagement, and to a close fight with their weapons. In which battle Demetrius was the conqueror, although Alexander's mercenaries shewed the greatest exploits, both in soul and body. Yet did the upshot of this battle prove different from what was expected, as to both of them; for neither did those that invited Demetrius to come to them continue firm to him, though he was conqueror; and six thousand Jews, out of pity to the change of Alexander's condition, when he was fled to the mountains, came over to him. Yet could not Demetrius bear this turn of affairs; but, supposing that Alexander was already become a match for him again, and that all the nation would [at length] run to him, left the country, and went his way.

However, the rest of the [Jewish] multitude did not lay aside their quarrels with him, when the [foreign] auxiliaries were gone; but they had a perpetual war with Alexander, until he had slain the greatest part of them, and driven the rest into the city Bemeselis; and when he had demolished that city, he carried the captives to Jerusalem. Nay, his rage was grown so extravagant, that his barbarity proceeded to a degree of impiety; for when he had ordered eight hundred to be hung upon crosses in the midst of the city, he had the throats of their wives and children cut before their eyes; and these executions he saw as he was drinking and lying down with his concubines. Upon which, so deep a surprise seized on the people, that eight thousand of his opposers fled away the very next night, out of all Judaea, whose flight was only terminated by Alexander's death; so at last, though not till late, and with great difficulty, he, by such actions, procured quiet to his kingdom, and left off fighting any more.[1]

In the parallel description in *Antiquities of the Jews* Josephus adds that, owing to his cruel deeds, Alexander Jannaeus was called by the Jews 'Thrakidan', the exact meaning of which is unknown; but it may be presumed to mean 'the Thracian', i.e., the man from Thrace, indicative of cruelty. Before Allegro published the Commentary, there were rumours, much publicized, that the word Thracian appeared in that Commentary with reference to the Wicked Priest. Now it is clear that this was completely groundless, except for Allegro's hint that possibly the Lion of Wrath was somehow connected with the Thracian, a suggestion which seems to us to be somewhat thin.

Nevertheless, we must confess that the resemblance between the description of events by Josephus and the description in the Commentary is startling. We can therefore infer that the name 'Seekers-after-Smooth-Things' (recurrent in the writings of the sect) actually refers to the Pharisees, who were the ones to invite Demetrius, an action which the sect—in spite of its opposition to Jannaeus—reviled, as can be learned from the Commentary.

The Commentary throws further light on the revolt, by mentioning that Demetrius, after his victory in Shechem, wished to conquer Jerusalem. And it is possibly this fact—suggested by Allegro—which brought about Demetrius' desertion by the Jews who had fought with him against Alexander. The latter's cruelty following the revolt, the ex-

[1] *The Wars of the Jews*, I, iv, 4, 5, 6.

pulsions and the many escapes, all created a period of disturbance and unrest, which fits many of the descriptions in the Commentaries.[1]

But who was the Teacher of Righteousness, leader of the sect and the main object of persecution by the Wicked Priest? Here again, scholars are divided according to their theories about the sect and its date, and we have no way of identifying him with certainty. We must again be satisfied with the facts about him in the Habakkuk Commentary and the Damascus Covenant. We know he was a priest endowed with the ability to interpret prophecies and to foretell the future events of his people. The Teacher of Righteousness was persecuted by his foes from inside and outside, and was compelled to flee and live in 'the house of exile'. We have already quoted the passage in the Damascus Covenant which says that 'He raised up for them a Teacher of Righteousness to lead them in the way of His heart'. According to the Damascus Covenant this happened some 410 years after they were exiled by Nebuchadnezzar, King of Babylon.

It seems evident, therefore, that to establish the date of compilation of the Habakkuk Commentary, we must first determine who were the Kittim. It is important to bear in mind that neither the Wicked Priest nor the Teacher of Righteousness (and the persecution of the sect) is mentioned in the scroll of The War of the Sons of Light against the Sons of Darkness; and second, that the Kittim, who play quite an important part in the Habakkuk Scroll (since it is they who will punish the Priests of Jerusalem) and are referred to always in a future tense, play the principal role in the War Scroll amongst the enemies of the Sons of Light; the fight against them is the fiercest of all. Elsewhere these Kittim are

[1] However, it is worth while warning the reader, that the identification of Demetrius with Demetrius III, as suggested by Allegro (a suggestion which I am inclined to accept), has most recently been challenged by Prof. Rowley of Manchester University. Rowley's suggestion is to identify him rather with Demetrius I (second century BC), who, according to I Maccabees, attempted to get possession of Jerusalem with the aid of a party of Jews.

called the 'Kittim of Asshur', and since, quite close to this passage, the 'Kittim in Egypt' are also mentioned, some scholars assumed that the Kittim in the War Scroll are the Seleucids and the 'Kittim in Egypt' the Ptolemies, i.e., the Greeks from north and south. We must, however, remember that the addition of Asshur to the word Kittim is not decisive for their identification. For in the same way as the author of Habakkuk used that word to refer to the Chaldeans, so the author of the War Scroll could have added the word Asshur if he had wanted to apply some of the Biblical prophecies on Asshur to the Kittim of his time; all the more so as the Bible often mentions Asshur close to or even together with Kittim.

We have read that the final battle between the Sons of Light and Darkness will culminate with a miracle in which the Sons of Light will wake up to find the Kittim dead. Here the hint is quite obvious: it reflects the miracle which happened when the army of Sennacherib of Asshur (Assyria) was smitten by the Angel, and the author of the scroll literally quotes Isaiah in saying: 'Then shall Asshur fall with the sword, not of man; and the sword not of man shall devour him.' To sum up, the word Asshur here in conjunction with the Kittim, does not help much in their identification. The author simply applies the quotation from Isaiah to what may happen to the Kittim of his time. The only conclusion to be derived from the fact that the Kittim in Egypt are also mentioned is that, in the author's time, Egypt was perhaps also under the rule of the Kittim.

But when determining the period of compilation of the War Scroll, there is one important factor to consider, exclusive to that scroll—namely the description of the army organization, the trumpets, the banners, the weapons, and the tactics. We can assume that even if the author made generous use of his imagination, he could not but be influenced by the fighting customs of his times—whether he had experienced them himself, heard about them from others, or read about them in some contemporary manual.

In a book on the scroll of the War of the Sons of Light against the Sons of Darkness,[1] I explained in detail how I reached the conclusion, on the basis of these military descriptions, that the scroll was compiled when Roman and not Hellenistic fighting customs were prevalent. My detailed reasoning is too lengthy for repetition here. It will be enough to record that the tactical principles and the weapons used were very similar to those of the Romans, and completely different from those of the Hellenistic armies. Examples are the use of signa and trumpets in battle, the rectangular shield of the heavy infantry which resembled the Roman scutum, the wearing of leggings by the riders alone, the size and shape of the sword, the lack of chariots and elephants, the use of 'intervals' (i.e., the tactical opening within the battle line), the number of fighters, the existence of reserve units. All these are typical of the Roman army. If this conclusion is correct, one can assume the War Scroll to have been written in the latter half of the first century BC. One can add, though with less certainty, that this scroll was compiled after the Habakkuk Commentary, since the internal troubles which weighed so heavily on the author of the latter—such as the persecution of the Teacher of Righteousness—are no more mentioned in the War Scroll. Here the persecution by the Kittim is the main theme, and they are the main enemies. Another aid would be the fact—as already explained—that the Kittim in the Habakkuk and Nahum Commentaries are referred to in the future tense.

Fixing the date of the other scrolls, such as the Thanksgiving hymns and the Manual of Discipline, is even more difficult, since they do not—like the Habakkuk and Nahum Commentaries—contain the slightest historical hint which could serve as a clue. The War Scroll, however, has descriptions of ceremonies and entire passages which appear in the Thanksgiving hymns and, in even greater detail, in the

[1] Published in Hebrew in 1955 by Mosad Bialik. The English translation is about to be published by the Clarendon Press, Oxford.

Manual of Discipline. Theoretically, then, the logical inference is that the two last-mentioned scrolls pre-date the War
Scroll. But an equally logical assumption is that all three
based their descriptions on an even earlier source unknown
to us. For the moment, with the data we have so far, the more
acceptable supposition is that the War Scroll is the latest of
these three.

To sum up, then, all archaeological and palaeographical
proofs indicate that the scrolls were copied and hidden during
the first century BC or the first half of the first century AD.
It appears, too, that the non-Biblical scrolls amongst the
documents that were found were also compiled within these
time limits, though not necessarily simultaneously.

We can now turn to the second problem associated with the
Dead Sea Scrolls: who were the people who lived in the
neighbourhood of Khirbet Qumran, wrote the scrolls and hid
them in the caves? Here, too, scholars are divided in their
opinion. And there is hardly a sect in Judaism or early Christianity which has not already been identified with the sect of
the scrolls. Let us therefore, before going into further analysis,
sum up what we know about the Dead Sea sect from its own
writings as to its beliefs, its political views and its organization.

The sect is opposed to the unification of the priesthood and
the kingship in one person. It believes that the lay leader
should be a descendant of the House of David, and the
religious head a descendant of the Sons of Zadok of the
House of Aaron. This is the ideal to which they aspire 'in
the end of the days'. One of the sentences in the writings of the sect is 'until there shall come a prophet and the
anointed ones of Aaron and Israel'. ('Anointed one' means
'Messiah'.) In the Damascus Covenant we sometimes find a
shorter formula for the same words: 'The anointed of Aaron
and Israel', which some scholars interpreted as meaning *one
anointed*, a descendant of both Aaron and Israel. This interpretation provoked many extreme theories. However, the

quotation from the Manual of Discipline is quite clearly a reference to two anointed ones, religious and lay, the one from Aaron, the other from Israel. Further evidence to prove that two anointed ones are meant is found in the War Scroll, as well as in some pages discovered later and belonging to the Manual of Discipline. This doctrine of the sect makes an interesting comparison with the custom prevalent in Hasmonean times, when some of the Hasmonean kings combined the crown of kingship and the crown of priesthood in their own person.

The sect, following its particular interpretation of the first chapter of Genesis, kept a three hundred and sixty-four day calendar, based on the solar months of thirty days, with an additional four inter-calary days, one after every three months. They could thus obviously not follow the calendar in use in Jerusalem, which was a lunar calendar. As a result their festivals occurred on different days. They could therefore not partake in the holy service in the Temple, where the official calendar was observed. They could not for the same reason sacrifice offerings. We have already learnt that one of the reasons why the sect was persecuted was that it celebrated its festivals, especially the Day of Atonement, on dates differing from the official calendar.

The deeds and thoughts of the sect were guided by the Law of Moses. They are most orthodox in adhering to the rules of the Torah, and their interpretation of its laws is far more strict than was customary in Jerusalem at the time. Part of their daily life is devoted to studying the Pentateuch. The sect does not oppose the marriage of its members, but it is quite clear from its writings that their rules of personal status were extremely rigid and the Manual of Discipline even indicates that within the sect itself there were groups of members who refrained from marrying.

Members of the sect attached particular importance to cleanliness of soul and body. This is evidenced in all their writings. They believe that everything has been pre-ordained, and that all creatures are divided into the Lot of Light and the Lot of Darkness. God himself has created Belial the Angel of Darkness, to lead all the forces of darkness. And he has also created Michael, the Angel of Light, to lead the forces of light. The difference between the Sons of Darkness and the Sons of Light is that, while the Sons of Darkness are entirely dependent upon the Angel of Darkness, the Sons of Light are actually within the Lot of God Himself, who fights their battle against the Sons of Darkness through the Angel of Light. This has been described in greater detail in the chapter discussing the War Scroll. The sect, accordingly, had considerably developed beliefs about angels and their part in battle, which may account for the fact that the names of the angels were inscribed on their battle shields.

They place great emphasis on knowledge and wisdom, with whose help they study the phenomena of the world and learn the secrets of creation. The words 'truth', 'justice' and 'judgement', which appear often on their standards, represent their principal beliefs. They are certain of the imminence of the victory of the Sons of Light over the Sons of Darkness. It will occur on the day pre-ordained by God. On that day, however, they will be compelled to fight bitterly: but until that day they must not take part in any wars, since these will not have been pre-ordained by God. In other words, one may interpret their daily behaviour and their attitude towards war generally during their time as being opposed to fighting. On the other hand they must be prepared for the day of vengeance; until then they must behave with patience. In the Manual of Discipline there is one significant passage on this point:

These are the regulations of the way for the wise man in these times [the times in which they live] for his love together with his hate, eternal hate for the men of the pit, in a spirit of concealment, leaving to them wealth and manual labour like a slave for the man who rules over him. Each one must be zealous for the law and be prepared and alert to the day of vengeance.

The sect rejects city life and its members live out of bounds. As far as concerns the members of the Dead Sea area, we know from their writings that they were organized in military fashion, and led a communal life devoid of individual possesssions; newcomers swore to give the *Yahad*, or community, their 'wealth, wisdom and strength'. They are divided into groups in order of seniority, and the younger must obey the older. Severe punishments are inflicted on transgressors of all kinds, whether against religious belief or against daily behaviour. Mention has already been made of the punishment for spitting in public, for example.

They have special rules for promotion and demotion in seniority. They eat together and follow a ceremonial pattern reminiscent of the ceremonies of sacrifices and offerings, with the priest officiating and uttering a special blessing. They have special functionaries such as supervisors and judges, whose duties are clearly laid down and who must be obeyed. The sect comprises Priests, Levites and Israelites. During ceremonies they dress themselves according to seniority, bear appropriate standards, perhaps blow trumpets, and generally try to resemble as far as possible the organization of the Tribes of Israel in the wilderness. They lead a life of modesty and fanatical orthodoxy, and spend their days studying the Bible and interpreting it. They prepare codes and rules for their way of life in the future, and wait patiently for the day of vengeance against all enemies of the Sons of Light.

Who were these people then? And what was the sect to which they belonged?

Sukenik was the first who suggested the identification of the sect with the Essenes. This suggestion was later accepted by many scholars who developed and sought to substantiate it. True or not, we cannot but recognize the striking similarity between what is known from the scrolls of the Dead Sea sect and what is known about the Essenes from the three main sources in existence: Philo of Alexandria, Josephus and Pliny (in his *Naturalis Historia*). Let us quote some of the relevant passages, so that the reader may judge the resemblance for himself. It is well to start with Josephus, possibly our most important source on the Essenes, their organization and way of life. In his *The Wars of the Jews*, Book II, Chapter 8, 2-10, 12-13, Josephus writes:

2. For there are three philosophical sects among the Jews. The followers of the first of whom are the Pharisees; of the second the Sadducees; and the third sect, who pretend to a severer discipline, are called Essenes. These last are Jews by birth, and seem to have a greater affection for one another than the other sects have. These Essenes reject pleasures as an evil, but esteem continence, and the conquest over our passions, to be virtue. They neglect wedlock, but choose out other persons' children, while they are pliable, and fit for learning; and esteem them to be of their kindred, and form them according to their own manners. They do not absolutely deny the fitness of marriage, and the succession of mankind thereby continued; but they guard against the lascivious behaviour of women, and are persuaded that none of them preserve their fidelity to one man.

3. These men are despisers of riches, and so very communicative as raises our admiration. Nor is there any one to be found among them who hath more than another; for it is a law among them, that those who come to them must let what they have be common to the whole order,—insomuch, that among them all there is no appearance of poverty or excess of riches, but every one's possessions are intermingled with every other's possessions; and so there is, as it were, one patrimony among all the brethren. They think that oil is a defilement; and if one of them be anointed without his own approbation, it is wiped off his body; for they think to be sweaty is a good thing, as they do also to be clothed in white garments. They also have stewards [supervisors] appointed to take care of their common affairs, who every one of them have no separate business for any, but what is for the use of them all.

4. They have no certain city, but many of them dwell in every city; and if any of their sect come from other places, what they have lies open for them, just as if it were their own; and they go into such as they never knew before, as if they had been ever so long acquainted with them. For which reason they carry nothing with

them when they travel into remote parts, though still they take their weapons with them, for fear of thieves. Accordingly there is, in every city where they live, one appointed particularly to take care of strangers, and provide garments and other necessaries for them. But the habit and management of their bodies are such as children use who are in fear of their masters. Nor do they allow of the change of garments, or of shoes, till they be first entirely torn to pieces, or worn out by time. Nor do they either buy or sell anything to one another; but every one of them gives what he hath to him that wanteth it, and receives from him again in lieu of it what it may be convenient for himself; and although there be no requital made, they are fully allowed to take what they want of whomsoever they please.

5. And as for their piety towards God, it is very extraordinary; for before sunrising they speak not a word about profane matters, but put up certain prayers which they have received from their forefathers, as if they made supplication for its rising. After this every one of them are sent away by their curators, to exercise some of those arts wherein they are skilled, in which they labour with great diligence till the fifth hour. After which they assemble themselves together again into one place; and when they have clothed themselves in white veils, they then bathe their bodies in cold water. And after this purification is over, they every one meet together in an apartment of their own, into which it is not permitted to any of another sect to enter; while they go, after a pure manner, into the dining-room as into a certain holy temple, and quietly set themselves down; upon which the baker lays them loaves in order; the cook also brings a single plate of one sort of food, and sets it before every one of them; but a priest says grace before meat; and it is unlawful for any one to taste of the food before grace be said. The same priest when he hath dined, says grace again after meat; and when they begin, and when they end, they praise God, as He that bestows their food upon them; after which they lay aside their [white] garments, and betake themselves to their labours again till the evening; they then return home to supper, after the same manner; and if there be any strangers there, they sit down with them. Nor is there ever any clamour or disturbance to pollute their house, but they give every one leave to speak in their turn; which silence thus kept in their house appears

to foreigners like some tremendous mystery; the cause of which is that perpetual sobriety they exercise, and some settled measure of meat and drink that is allotted to them, and that such as is abundantly sufficient for them.

6. And truly, as for other things, they do nothing but according to the injunctions of their curators; only these two things are done among them at every one's own free will, which are, to assist those that want it, and to show mercy; for they are permitted of their own accord to afford succour to such as deserve it, when they stand in need of it, and to bestow food on those that are in distress; but they cannot give anything to their kindred without the curators. They dispense their anger after a just manner, and restrain their passion. They are eminent for fidelity, and are the ministers of peace; whatsoever they say also is firmer than an oath; but swearing is avoided by them, and they esteem it worse than perjury; for they say, that he who cannot be believed without [swearing by] God, is already condemned. They also take great pains in studying the writings of the ancients, and choose out of them what is most for the advantage of their soul and body; and they inquire after such roots and medicinal stones as may cure their distempers.

7. But now, if any one hath a mind to come over to their sect, he is not immediately admitted, but he is prescribed the same method of living which they use, for a year, while he continues excluded; and they give him a small hatchet, and the forementioned girdle, and the white garment. And when he hath given evidence, during that time, that he can observe their continence, he approaches nearer to their way of living, and is made a partaker of the waters of purification; yet is he not even now admitted to live with them; for after this demonstration of his fortitude, his temper is tried two more years, and if he appear to be worthy, they then admit him into their society. And before he is allowed to touch their common food, he is obliged to take tremendous oaths, that, in the first place, he will exercise piety towards God; and then, that he will observe justice towards all men; and that he will do no harm to any one, either of his own accord, or by the command of others; that he will always hate the wicked, and be assistant to the righteous; that he will ever show fidelity to all men, and especially to those in authority, he will at no time whatever abuse his auth-

ority, nor endeavour to outshine his subjects, either in his garments, or any other finery; that he will be perpetually a lover of truth, and propose to himself to reprove those that tell lies; that he will keep his hands clear from theft, and his soul from unlawful gains; and that he will neither conceal anything from those of his own sect, nor discover any of their doctrines to others, no, not though any one should compel him so to do at the hazard of his life. Moreover, he swears to communicate their doctrines to no one any otherwise than as he received them himself; that he will abstain from robbery, and will equally preserve the books belonging to their sect, and the names of the angels [or messengers]. These are the oaths by which they secure their proselytes to themselves.

8. But for those that are caught in any heinous sins, they cast them out of their society; and he who is thus separated from them, does often die after a miserable manner; for as he is bound by the oath he hath taken, and by the customs he hath been engaged in, he is not at liberty to partake of that food that he meets with elsewhere, but is forced to eat grass, and to famish his body with hunger till he perish; for which reason they receive many of them, again when they are at their last gasp, out of compassion to them as thinking the miseries they have endured till they come to the very brink of death to be a sufficient punishment for the sins they had been guilty of.

9. But in the judgements they exercise they are most accurate and just; nor do they pass sentence by the votes of a court that is fewer than a hundred. And as to what is once determined by that number, it is unalterable. What they most of all honour, after God Himself, is the name of their legislator [Moses]; whom, if any one blaspheme, he is punished capitally. They also think it a good thing to obey their elders, and the major part. Accordingly, if ten of them be sitting together, no one of them will speak while the other nine are against it. They also avoid spitting in the midst of them, or on the right side. Moreover, they are stricter than any other of the Jews in resting from their labours on the seventh day; for they not only get their food ready the day before, that they may not be obliged to kindle a fire on that day, but they will not remove any vessel out of its place, nor go to stool thereon. Nay, on the other days they dig a small pit, a foot deep, with a paddle (which kind of

hatchet is given them when they are first admitted among them); and covering themselves round with their garment, that they may not affront the divine rays of light, they ease themselves into that pit, after which they put the earth that was dug out again into the pit; and even this they do only in the more lonely places, which they choose out for this purpose; and although this easement of the body be natural, yet it is a rule with them to wash themselves after it, as if it were a defilement to them.

10. Now after the time of their preparatory trial is over, they are parted into four classes; and so far are the juniors inferior to the seniors, that if the seniors should be touched by the juniors, they must wash themselves, as if they had intermixed themselves with the company of a foreigner. They are long-lived also; insomuch that many of them live above a hundred years, by means of the simplicity of their diet; nay, as I think, by means of the regular course of life they observe also. They contemn the miseries of life, and are above pain, by the generosity of their mind. And as for death, if it will be for their glory, they esteem it better than living always; and indeed our war with the Romans gave abundant evidences what great souls they had in their trials, wherein, although they were tortured and distorted, burnt and torn to pieces, and went through all kinds of instruments of torment, that they might be forced either to blaspheme their legislator or to eat what was forbidden them, yet could they not be made to do either of them, no, nor once to flatter their tormentors, nor to shed a tear; but they smiled in their very pains, and laughed those to scorn who inflicted the torments upon them, and resigned up their souls with great alacrity, as expecting to receive them again. . . .

12. There are also among them who undertake to foretell things to come, by reading the holy books, and using several sorts of purifications, and being perpetually conversant in the discourses of the prophets; and it is but seldom that they miss in their predictions.

13. Moreover, there is another order of Essenes, who agree with the rest as to their way of living, and customs, and laws, but differ from them in the point of marriage, as thinking that by not marrying they cut off the principal part of human life, which is the prospect of succession; nay rather, that if all men should be of the same opinion, the whole race of mankind would fail. However,

they try their spouses for three years; and if they find that they have their natural purgations thrice, as trials that they are likely to be fruitful, they then actually marry them. But they do not use to accompany with their wives when they are with child, as a demonstration that they do not marry out of regard to pleasure, but for the sake of posterity. Now the women go into the baths with some of their garments on, as the men do with somewhat girded about them. And these are the customs of this order of Essenes.

This description shows the evident similarity between the Essenes and the Dead Sea sect. The Essenes avoid a life of wealth, and share all belongings (cf. the Manual of Discipline). They do not concentrate in one place of dwelling but live in scattered camps. The Manual of Discipline tells of punishment for those who speak out of turn and Josephus, writing of the Essenes, says: 'They give every one leave to speak in their turn . . .' That the Essenes will do nothing without the express order of their curators, that new members are not accepted unless first going through a period of probation, is also similar to what we have learned of the Dead Sea sect. Many of the parallels are striking.

The next important source of details about the Essenes is Philo in Chapter 12 of his book *Every good Man is Free* (*Quod omnis probus liber*). Compared with the writing of Josephus, who knew the Essenes well and even spent some time with them in his youth, Philo's words read as if they are written at second hand. Discrepancies between his account of the Essenes and of what we know of the sect do not necessarily discount their identification, since similarly there are discrepancies between Philo's account of the Essenes and Josephus's account. Philo writes:

Palestinian Syria, too, has not failed to produce high moral excellence. In this country live a considerable part of the very populous nation of the Jews, including, as it is said, certain persons more than four thousand in number, called Essenes. Their name which is, I think, a variation, though the form of the Greek is inexact, of ὁσεότης (holiness) is given them, because they have shown themselves especially devout in the service of God, not by offering sacrifices of animals, but by resolving to sanctify their minds. The first thing about these people is that they live in villages and avoid the cities because of the iniquities which have become inveterate among city dwellers, for they know that their company would have a deadly effect upon their own souls, like a disease brought by a pestilential atmosphere. Some of them labour on the land and others pursue such crafts as co-operate with peace and so benefit themselves and their neighbours. They do not hoard gold and silver or acquire great slices of land because they desire the revenues therefrom, but provide what is needed for the necessary requirements of life. For while they stand almost alone in the whole of mankind in that they have become moneyless and landless by deliberate action rather than by lack of good fortune, they are esteemed exceedingly rich, because they judge frugality with contentment to be, as indeed it is, an abundance of wealth. As for darts, javelins, daggers or the helmet, breastplate or shield, you could not find a single manufacturer of them, nor, in general, any person making weapons or engines or plying any industry concerned with war, nor indeed any of the peaceful kind, which easily lapse into vice, for they have not the vaguest idea of commerce either wholesale or retail or marine, but pack the inducements to covetousness off in disgrace. Not a single slave is to be found among them, but all are free, exchanging services with each other, and they denounce the owners of slaves not merely for their impiety in annulling the statute of Nature, who mother-like has borne and reared all men alike and created them genuine brothers, not in mere name, but in very reality, though this kinship has been put to confusion by the triumph of malignant covetousness, which has wrought estrangement instead of affinity and enmity instead of friendship. As for philosophy they abandon the logical part to quibbling verbalists as unnecessary for the acquisition of virtue, and the physical to visionary praters as beyond the grasp of human nature, only retaining that part which treats philosophically of the existence of God and the creation of the universe. But the ethical part they study very industriously, taking for their trainers the laws of their fathers, which could not possibly have been conceived by the human soul without divine inspiration.

In these they are instructed at all other times, but particularly on the seventh day. For that day has been set apart to be kept holy and on it they abstain from all other work and proceed to sacred spots which they call synagogues. There arranged in rows according to their ages, the younger below the elder, they sit decorously as befits the occasion with attentive ears. Then one takes the books and reads aloud and another of especial proficiency comes forward and expounds what is not understood. For most of their philosophical study takes the form of allegory, and in this they emulate the tradition of the past. They are trained in piety, holiness, justice, domestic and civic conduct, knowledge of what is truly good, or evil, or indifferent, and how to choose what they should and avoid the opposite, taking for their defining standards these three, love of God, love of virtue, love of men. Their love of God they show by a multitude of proofs, by religious purity constant and unbroken throughout their lives, by abstinence from oaths, by veracity, by their belief that the Godhead is the cause of all good things and nothing bad; their love of virtue, by their freedom from the love of either money or reputation or pleasure, by self-mastery and endurance, again by frugality, simple living, contentment, humility, respect for law, steadiness and all similar qualities; their love of men by benevolence and sense of equality, and their spirit of fellowship, which defies description, though a few words on it will not be out of place. First of all then no one's house is his own in the sense that it is not shared by all, for besides the fact that they dwell together in communities, the door is open to visitors from elsewhere who share their convictions. Again they all have a single treasury and common disbursements; their clothes are held in common and also their food through their institution of public meals. In no other community can we find the custom of sharing roof, life and board more firmly established in actual practice, and that is no more than one would expect. For all the wages which they earn in the day's work, they do not keep as their private property but throw them into the common stock and allow the benefit thus accruing to be shared by those who wish to use it. The sick are not neglected because they cannot provide anything, but have the cost of their treatment lying ready in the common stock, so that they can meet expenses out of the greater wealth in full security. To the elder men too is given the respect and care which real children give to their parents, and they receive from countless hands and minds a full and generous maintenance for their latter years.

There remains now the question of whether the Essenes lived on the shores of the Dead Sea or in Khirbet Qumran itself, where the public building of the Scrolls sect was found. Pliny in his Natural History gives us interesting information on that score:

On the west side of the Dead Sea but out of range of the noxious exhalations of the coast, is the solitary tribe of the Essenes, which is remarkable beyond all the other tribes in the whole world, as it has no women and has renounced all sexual desire, has no money, and has only palm-trees for company. Day by day the throng of refugees is recruited to an equal number by numerous accessions of persons tired of life and driven thither by the waves of fortune to adopt their manners. Thus through thousands of ages (incredible to relate) a race in which no one is born lives on for ever; so prolific for their advantage is other men's weariness of life.

Lying below the Essenes was formerly the town of Engedi, second only to Jerusalem in the fertility of its land and in its groves of palm-trees, but now like Jerusalem a heap of ashes. Next comes Masada, a fortress on a rock, itself also not far from the Dead Sea. This is the limit of Judaea.

The above passage from Pliny, who died in the year AD 79, is most significant; first he specifies clearly that the Essenes of whom he is writing lived on the western shore of the Dead Sea. From his description of Engedi as lying 'below the Essenes' it may mean either that the town of the Essenes was in the hills above Engedi, or—as Dupont-Sommer suggests with justice—that Engedi lay south of the Essene settlement. The latter is the more reasonable, since after mentioning Engedi, Pliny proceeds to say 'next comes Masada'. In other words, he is enumerating the places from north to south.

We therefore have before us two alternative conclusions: either the sect of the Scrolls is none other than the Essenes themselves; or it was a sect which resembled the Essenes in almost every respect, its dwelling place, its organization, its customs. It may sound strange that today we actually know more about the sect of the Scrolls than we do about the Essenes. Even the Essenes' Hebrew name—which is only given in Greek or Latin—is as yet unknown to us.

Space does not allow us to record all the opinions of the various scholars on the identification of the sect with one or another historical sect. But perhaps it is of interest to mention the extreme opinion expressed by Dr Teicher, of the University of Cambridge, who believes the sect to have been the Ebionites, the Jewish-Christian sect of early Christianity. I mention this view not because I agree with Dr Teicher, but because his opinion has found some support in certain circles. Teicher argues *inter alia* that the fact that the word 'Ebionites' (literally 'the poor') is repeated several times in the writings of the sect in reference to its members proves that they are none other than the Judaeo-Christians, that is the sect founded immediately following the crucifixion of Jesus, who were referred to as Ebionites (i.e., 'the poor in spirit'). It is known that members of that sect were Jews in all principles, customs and beliefs, except one—they believed Jesus to have been the Messiah.

The efforts of the Apostle Paul to spread the Christian faith outside the boundaries of Palestine, and the difficulties he encountered in his activities in imposing the Mosaic Law, compelled him to sever his connexions with the Ebionites and to take the view, as Dupont-Sommer put it, 'that the law was decadent and outworn and that the faithful followers of Christ were no longer bound by it.'

It is easy to understand that his clashes with the Ebionites would be serious. When the country was conquered by Roman invaders, the Ebionites had to flee. They found refuge in the Trans-Jordan. The destruction of the Temple was also a death-blow to the Ebionites, and brought about an end to the experiment of a Jewish-Christian sect.

Teicher identifies the Teacher of Righteousness with Jesus and the Wicked Priest with the Apostle Paul. It is clear therefore that he also maintains that the date of the writing of the scrolls was later than the date of the destruction of the Temple. It is difficult to accept this theory for the archaeological, palaeographical, and chronological reasons we have outlined above, and for still other reasons which point to some of the basic differences between the teachings and customs of the sect and those of early Christianity.

However, the fact that a scholar like Teicher suggests the identification of the Dead Sea sect with the Judaeo-Christians, and bases himself also on the resemblance between some of the opinions and ceremonies enumerated in the scrolls and several ancient Christian documents certainly shows that there are some similarities between the two. However, while a resemblance between the two does exist, the opposite interpretation has greater validity. In other words, the early Christians were influenced by the views of the people of this sect, which in many ways suited their own opinions. Long before the discovery of the Dead Sea Scrolls, many scholars recognized the connexion between John the Baptist and the Essenes, as described in the writings of Josephus, Philo and Pliny, especially since John is known to have lived and preached in the actual vicinity of Khirbet Qumran. This is what the Gospel according to St Matthew says:

And in those days came John the Baptist, preaching in the Wilderness of Judaea, and saying, Repent ye: for the kingdom of heaven is at hand. For this is he that was spoken of by the prophet Esaias, saying, The voice of one crying in the wilderness, Prepare ye the way of the Lord, make his paths straight. And the same John had his raiment of camel's hair, and a leathern girdle about his loins; and his meat was locusts and wild honey. Then went out to him Jerusalem, and all Judaea, and all the region round about Jordan, And were baptized of him in the Jordan, confessing their sins. [iii, 1–6].

In the chapter on the Manual of Discipline I mentioned

that John the Baptist quotes the sentence in Isaiah which is also quoted in the Manual of Discipline:

And when those will form themselves as a *Yahad* [Community] in Israel according to these rules, they shall be separated from the midst of the session of the men of evil to go to the wilderness to prepare there His way as it is written: In the wilderness prepare the way [of the Lord], make straight in the desert a highway for our God.

* * *

Any attempt at this stage of research to identify the Dead Sea sect with any other sect of the time is more likely to be based on assumptions than on facts. In the last centuries before the destruction of the Temple, there were more different persecuted sects and groups than in any other period in the history of Judaism. But this is just what gives prime significance to the Dead Sea Scrolls; they were written during a decisive period in the history of the Jewish people, and on the eve of the birth of Christianity. For the first time today we have comprehensive documents—including Biblical books, codes of a sect and contemporary literary products— which shed new and important light on the problems of Biblical texts, of the Hebrew and Aramaic languages, and on the beliefs and organization of one of the most astonishing religious sects that ever existed. We now have a new basis for the clarification and elucidation of some of the facts concerning the foundation of Christianity, and especially of the influence of Judaism on the Christian faith. In each of these fields the commonplaces of scholarship are up for re-examination in the light of the new material offered by the scrolls.

Research on the scrolls is still in its initial stages. For one thing most of the scrolls, though discovered several years back, have only recently been published, so that scholars have not yet had much time to examine them thoroughly. For another, there are still thousands of fragments, unearthed after the initial discovery of the seven scrolls, which have not yet been published for the benefit of the scholarly world, and it is quite possible that, when they are, more data will be revealed which may help to solve some of the problems posed in these pages.

The tense drama of the discovery and acquisition of the scrolls, the high excitement of their deciphering, the sudden opening of a comparatively tiny window on to the life and customs of a remarkable group of people who had been lost to history—such is the story of the Dead Sea Scrolls up to now. It is far from over. The fruits of continued research on these scrolls will long affect the entire pattern of our knowledge and thought about the books of the Bible, and about the people who shaped their lives to their study.

Index

ABOUT THE AUTHOR

MAJOR GENERAL YIGAEL YADIN, like Lawrence of Arabia in another generation, has specialized in archaeology and soldiering. He became Chief of Staff of the Israeli Army at the age of thirty. During the Israeli-Arab war which broke out in 1948, he developed a strategy of desert warfare based partly on his study of the Bible and his research on campaigns described in the Old Testament. He is at present lecturer in archaeology at the Hebrew University of Jerusalem, and is currently in charge of the largest archaeological excavation in Israel, digging on the site of Hazor, the most important Canaanite city in Galilee, which was conquered by Joshua, another famous Jewish general, some 3,300 years ago.